Essential Histories

The Punic Wars
264–146 BC

Essential Histories

The Punic Wars
264–146 BC

Nigel Bagnall

First published in Great Britain in 2002 by Osprey Publishing,
Elms Court, Chapel Way, Botley, Oxford OX2 9LP

Email: info@ospreypublishing.com

ISBN 1 84176 355 1

Editor: Rebecca Cullen
Design: Ken Vail Graphic Design, Cambridge, UK
Cartography by The Map Studio
Index by Alan Thatcher
Picture research by Image Select International
Origination by Grasmere Digital Imaging, Leeds, UK
Printed and bound in China by L. Rex Printing Company Ltd.

02 03 04 05   10 9 8 7 6 5 4 3 2 1

For a complete list of titles available from Osprey Publishing
please contact:

Osprey Direct UK, PO Box 140,
Wellingborough, Northants, NN8 4ZA, UK
Email: info@ospreydirect.co.uk

Osprey Direct USA,
c/o Motorbooks International, PO Box 1,
Osceola, WI 54020-0001, USA.
Email: info@ospreydirectusa.com

www.ospreypublishing.com

Acknowledgements

I am grateful to Pimlico of Random House who have kindly
permitted me to draw on my book *The Punic Wars: Rome,
Carthage and the Struggle for the Mediterranean* (1999) which
gives a fuller account of the three wars. I am also grateful to my
old friend Major General David Alexander-Sinclair for his careful
reading of the Osprey manuscript and helpful comments.

I owe my wife Anna and my two daughters, Emma and Sarah, a
special word of thanks for their patience, tolerance and good
humour over the years and to whom I now dedicate this book.

Contents

Introduction

There are those who would have us believe that man is a peace-loving animal, asking for no more than to be allowed to live in harmony with his fellow beings, rearing his family and pursuing his interests in contented prosperity. Such aspirations are savagely disrupted by the excesses of power-hungry despots and their brutal soldiery. The pious then regard history as little more than a tragic record of how peace is shattered by a few evil men; while military history is dismissed as a corrupting influence, glorifying war and promoting xenophobia. Yet wars have never been intermittent occurrences disrupting the natural, orderly condition of man, but rather an activity pursued with relentless consistency, sometimes with relish, and under many different guises.

As Professor Sir Michael Howard said in his David Davies Memorial Institute lecture entitled Weapons and Peace (January 1983):

The causes of war are as diverse as those of human conflict itself, but one factor common to almost all wars has been on the one side, or both, a cultural predisposition for war, whether this has been confined to ruling elites, or widespread throughout society. This is a factor which has been so often overlooked by liberal-minded historians, the existence of cultures, almost universal in the past, far from extinct in our day, in which the settling of contentious issues by armed conflict is regarded as natural, inevitable and right.

However unpalatable, the realities surrounding war should be recognised. Rather than taking refuge in wishful thinking, to avoid wars we should investigate their causes, consider how they might be prevented and prepare to defend ourselves, in itself a powerful deterrent. The study of military history then provides some perspective and enables us to learn from the lessons of the past.

The Greek historian Polybius wrote: 'There are only two sources from which any benefit can be derived, our own misfortunes and those which have happened to other men.' Bearing these words in mind, we can turn to the three human misfortunes known as the Punic Wars which, in spite of their remoteness, possess a remarkable contemporary relevance. Two largely incompatible civilisations confronted one another in a rivalry that quickly became a to-the-death fight for supremacy. The lessons of that struggle clearly demonstrate the need for positive and consistent national policy, and the importance of co-ordinated land and naval operations; equally they highlight the consequences of failing to adapt military force structures and thinking to match circumstances, the impact of new technology (as exemplified by the *corvus*) and the relevance of certain battlefield principles which are common to any war.

The three Punic Wars, which lasted for more than 100 years in all, though with long periods of peace in-between, and extended throughout the Mediterranean were to decide the future of the Western world. The contest was between two races: the Indo-Germanic, which incorporated the Greeks and Romans, and the Semitic, which included the Jews and Arabs. The one side had a genius of order and legislation, the other the spirit of commercial adventure and a love of gold, blood and pleasure.

There are basically two different ways of presenting the wars that determined the course of European, if not world history: an across-the-board chronological account, or a sequential examination of the different campaigns, each in its entirety. The conventional method has been the former, but I have chosen the latter because I consider any difficulty in interrelating events occurring at the same time in different theatres to be far outweighed by the ability to follow through the development of each separate campaign. To support this approach the chronology at the end of this introduction presents the milestones of the wars and details of the events which led to Sicily becoming the principal battlefield of the First Punic War. Finally, there is a glossary of names of the principal characters.

Chronology

814 BC The founding of Carthage by Phoenician settlers from Tyre.

800 BC After some unknown natural catastrophe which decimated the population, Phoenician migrants return to Sicily, followed by Greeks.

750 BC The traditional date for the founding of Rome.

509 BC Treaty of friendship signed between Rome and Carthage defining trading rights.

415 BC Athenian expedition (during the Peloponnesian War) attempts to wrest Syracuse from the Spartans and cut their grain supplies from Sicily but is totally annihilated, leaving Doric Syracuse as the dominant and most prestigious city in Sicily.

480 BC Gelon of Syracuse defeats the Carthaginians at Himera and effectively removes their influence from the island for 70 years.

405 BC A resurgence of Carthaginian influence in Sicily leads to a second war with the Greek settlements, ending with the Carthaginians in possession of most of the western part of the island.

380 BC A second treaty is signed between Rome and Carthage confirming their respective trading rights.

310 BC In a third war between the Carthaginians and Greeks, Agathocles of Syracuse extends his domain in Sicily and lands in North Africa, marches on Carthage but being too weak to take the city, returns to Sicily.

290 BC Following the death of Agathocles, the Carthaginians attempt to reassert their domination but in 278 BC Pyrrhus, King of Epirus, crosses over to Sicily and secures most of the island until forced to leave through lack of support.

279 BC A third treaty is drawn up between Rome and Carthage. It confirms the earlier treaties and adds the significant clause that they would go to one another's assistance if attacked.

275 BC The Carthaginians regain most of Sicily.

264 BC The Romans intervene in Sicily and the First Punic War begins.

256 BC Carthaginian naval supremacy is broken at the battle of Ecnomus, enabling the Romans to land in North Africa where they are heavily defeated.

241 BC A new Carthaginian fleet is destroyed, which leads to the end of the First Punic War.

240 BC Disgruntled returning Carthaginian mercenaries revolt.

241 BC The Gauls invade Italy.

236 BC The Romans respond to a request from Carthaginian mercenaries and seize Sardinia.

237 BC Hamilcar Barca begins the conquest of Spain and establishes a Barcid empire.

229 BC Hamilcar is drowned when attempting to escape across a river. He is succeeded by his son-in-law Hasdrubal.

229 BC The Romans invade Illyria.

221 BC Hasdrubal is assassinated and following the army's unanimous choice, Hannibal is confirmed by Carthage as the new commander in Spain.

220 BC Saguntum is placed under Roman protection but taken by Hannibal, the last of many incidents leading inevitably to war.

218 BC Hannibal marches from Spain, crosses the Alps and invades Italy to begin the Second Punic War.

217 BC Hannibal defeats the Romans at Lake Trasimene.

216 BC Hannibal wins an annihilating victory at Cannae and the Romans go on the defensive, avoiding any major encounter.

215 BC The war expands to Spain, Sardinia, Sicily and Illyria.

211 BC After threatening Rome, Hannibal is in retreat and progressively confined to southern Italy.

207 BC Hannibal's brother Hasdrubal leaves Spain and crosses the Alps but is defeated and killed at the battle of Metaurus.

206 BC Scipio secures Spain.

205 BC Scipio lands in North Africa.

203 BC Hannibal is recalled to defend Carthage.

202 BC Scipio defeats Hannibal at Zama.

201 BC The Carthaginians accept the Roman Senate's peace terms confining them to their African territories, surrendering their fleet and paying a large indemnity of silver.

200 BC Polybius, who wrote the history of the Punic Wars, is born in Arcadia, a country in the centre of Peleponnesus, now a part of modern Greece.

155 BC Cato starts urging the Senate to renew hostilities against a rejuvenated Carthage which, he claims, poses a mortal threat to Rome.

149 BC The Carthaginians refuse a Roman ultimatum to surrender their city and the Third Punic War begins.

146 BC Carthage is captured and obliterated.

Two great Mediterranean powers

With hindsight it is hard not to conclude that war between Carthage and Rome had a degree of inevitability, but at the time there seemed no reason why this should be so. Rome had established its hegemony over the whole of the Italian peninsula only relatively recently and the Senate showed no inclination for further expansion, while Carthage had no territorial designs beyond the retention of her colonies and trading posts scattered around the Mediterranean

Gravestone from a children's cemetery. The Carthaginians practised the sacrifice of children. (Edimedia, Paris)

seaboard. In a later chapter I will examine how the conflict arose, but first let us take a closer look at the two protagonists, Carthage and Rome.

The classical sources only give us restricted information. The wars themselves are well covered but otherwise we only have sporadic data, such as what the Greek philosopher Aristotle, writing in the 4th century BC, has to say about the Carthaginian constitution, or the writings of Polybius on the Carthaginian Mercenary Revolt. Moreover, as Carthage was totally destroyed after the Third Punic War, in 146 BC, no records have survived. All we have are the results of archaeological excavations in cemeteries which, though providing much information about the minor arts (for example, terracotta figurines, carved ivory and jewellery, together with inscribed stelae bearing figures), tell us nothing about the human dramas that unfolded, or the day to day activities and concerns of the civilian population. It is much the same with the Romans of this period: records deal almost exclusively with the actual fighting, without any mention of, for example, how the women bore such stupendous losses amongst their menfolk or, indeed, how they themselves aided the war effort.

Carthage

Founding

It was Phoenician settlers from Tyre, just north of today's border between Israel and Lebanon, who founded Carthage not far north of modern Tunis, in about 814 BC. According to one source, those who settled in Tyre were given the name Phoenician, meaning 'dark skinned' by the Greeks. Others maintain the name derived from the purple

dye, phonix, which was obtained from
molluscs of the *Murex* genus and used
extensively in the dyeing of linen or woollen
goods. For their part, the Romans called them
Poeni, which led to the name Punic. But
whatever their etymological origins, the
Phoenicians were a Semitic race and a
seafaring people who, according to Herodotus,
the Greek fifth-century BC historian known as
the 'Father of History', sailed down the Gulf,
round Africa and returned to the
Mediterranean through the Straits of Gibraltar
to establish a number of trading posts.
Amongst these, near the head of a sandstone
peninsula that provided shelter for both
warships and merchant vessels, was Carthage.
Though by far the largest city, there were
many others in North Africa, Spain, with its
rich gold, silver and copper mines, Sardinia,
Cyprus, Malta and – most importantly – Sicily,
where Carthaginian expansion was eventually
checked by Greek settlements in the east of
the island.

People

What is known about the Carthaginian
character comes from Roman sources and so
may not be altogether impartial. Polybius
refers to the more virtuous Roman attitude
towards money matters, whereby wealth
obtained by unlawful transactions was
widely disapproved of and bribery was
punished by death. The Carthaginians, on
the other hand, obtained office by open
bribery and nothing which resulted in profit
was thought disgraceful. Cicero, the first-
century AD Roman consul, orator and writer,
identified the Carthaginians' most
distinguishing characteristics as being craft,
skill, industry and cunning, all of which in
moderation can reasonably be associated
with people who made their living through
trade. Others allege, however, that the
Carthaginians combined these characteristics
to an inordinate degree. 'Punic honour' and
a 'Carthaginian mind' were derogatory terms
in Roman times. In spite of these
unflattering labels, it seems reasonable to
conclude that the Carthaginians were, like
all mortals, neither wholly good nor wholly

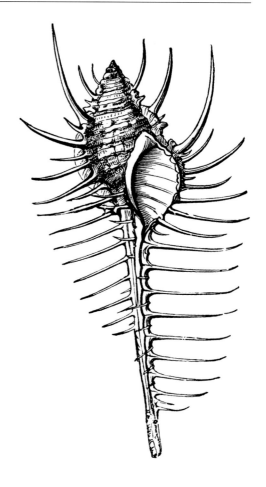

An example of a murex shell, from which purple dye can
be obtained. (Ann Ronan Picture Library)

bad. They were traders who lived by profit in
a time when their political institutions were
in decline and their religious practices a
cause for disgust, but their personal and
collective conduct might have appeared
corrupt to the Romans, who were at an
earlier, more austere and virtuous stage of
their evolutionary development.

Religion

References to the Phoenician religion and
that of Carthage in particular are
fragmentary and at times contradictory.
What we do know is that the Carthaginian
religion was polytheistic, characterised by
the worship of a number of deities who
controlled the totality of man's needs and
the needs of society. In this respect it is not

dissimilar to several other civilisations, with a pantheon of superhuman beings who had to be propitiated and placated in accordance with established rites. What was different, however, was the way in which the political independence of the city states enabled them to develop a diversity of religious interpretations. Each city organised its own form of worship, creating individual traditions, assigning prominence to a range of elected deities of their own choosing and attracting their own somewhat surprising customs. For example, Astarte, the Phoenician female warrior deity, was also connected with Aphrodite, or Venus, and her worship involved temple prostitution, a sexual ritual that slaves and other women fulfilled on payment, catering particularly for foreign visitors.

During the fifth century BC Carthage began to adopt an increasingly independent theology and liturgy. When relations with Tyre were broken off, the worship of Melquarth, Lord of the City, was replaced by that of Baal Hammon, and Astarte was renamed Tanit. These changes gave a sinister turn to Carthaginian religion since Baal Hannon had to be placated by human sacrifice. It was not, however, only the Carthaginians who followed such a practice, as is borne out by the biblical prophet Jeremiah, who relates how the children of Judah did evil in that they built topeths 'to burn their sons and daughters in the fire', a custom which was continued among the Canaanites and later by the Israelites.

There is considerable controversy as to the extent of human sacrifice. Some scholars maintain that it was fairly common, while others, especially archaeologists, now consider it to have been reserved for times of extreme danger, and suggest that the cremated remains of children found near all the Carthaginian settlements were usually of those who had died from sickness or other natural causes and had been 'offered' to the gods. Against this moderating interpretation must be set the barbarous description given by Diodorus Siculus, a first-century BC Greek historian: 'There was a brazen statue putting forth the

palms of its hands bending in such a manner towards the earth, so that the boy to be sacrificed who was laid upon them would roll off and fall into a deep fiery furnace.'

Though prisoners were also sacrificed, it seems unlikely that Carthaginian religious practices would have determined their conduct on the battlefield. Hannibal and others sacrificed animals to the gods before undertaking some hazardous enterprise, but that seems to have been about all.

Constitution

Although the other Phoenician cities each had their government, they were dependent on Carthage for defence as they had no military forces of their own. There was then no solid political unity or cohesion between them. It was the rather loose constitution as it affected the city states that certainly contributed to Carthage's downfall. As for the subject territories in Africa and Sardinia, they were made to pay tribute, and their discontent was reflected in the part they subsequently played in revolts. Carthage had merely created a feudal empire with no sense of corporate loyalty, whereas Rome, as we will see, had forged a confederation of states which, for the most part, held together even when gravely threatened

Despite this lack of cohesion, Cicero had this to say: 'Carthage could not have maintained her pre-eminent position for six hundred years had she not been governed with wisdom and statesmanship.' A rare tribute from a Roman at a time when the bitter legacies of the long struggle of the Punic Wars must still have been very much to the forefront of his compatriots' minds.

Though we know little about the circumstances in Carthage itself that produced such estimable results, they can to a large extent be attributed to the political stability provided by the aristocracy. The patriciate of Carthage was never as hereditary as that of early Rome, and the interminable constitutional struggles which racked the Roman political and social scene were relatively unknown in Carthage. Elevation to the aristocracy was by wealth,

The Carthaginian empire and dependencies

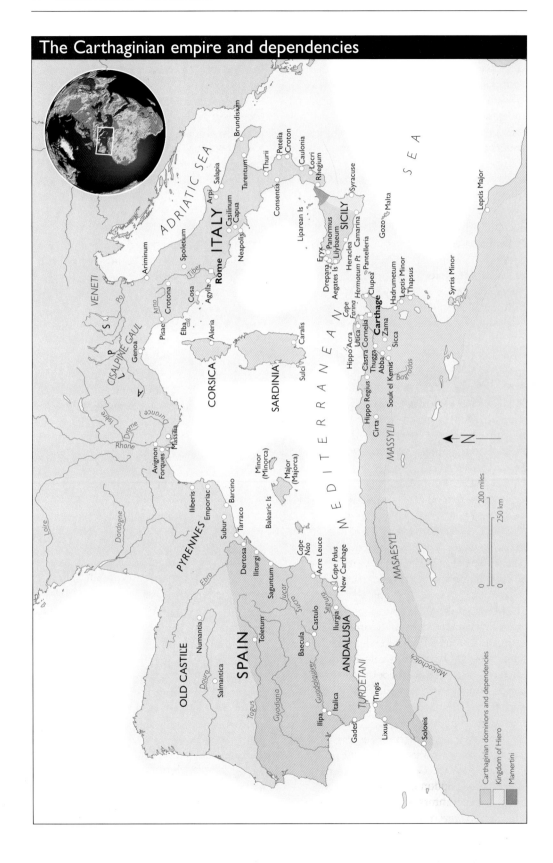

Carthaginian dominions and dependencies
Kingdom of Hiero
Mamertini

which ensured a steady flow of new, enterprising families who invigorated public life. This was offset, however, by widespread corruption: not only could the highest offices be purchased, but a return on this investment was demanded. As in any state, corrupt political leadership permeates all levels of society.

Rome

Founding

The development of Rome into a dominating power throughout the Italian peninsula happened over three broad periods. The first lasted from the traditional date of the city's founding in about 750 BC until its absorption by the Etruscans about 100 years later; the second period of Etruscan colonisation lasted some 250 years until around 400 BC; then, after its brief occupation by the Gauls in 386 BC, Rome's own expansion gradually began, so forming the third and final period of its growth. This was completed in 270 BC with the surrender of Rhegium (Reggio).

Though the earlier periods are of historic interest and relevant to our wider understanding of the Roman political, religious, cultural and economic customs and attitudes, we are only concerned with the final period of expansion and the subsequent development of Rome into a confederation.

As Rome had extended her hegemony, she had come into conflict with Greek cities scattered around the peninsula's southern coastlines. One of these cities, Tarentum (Taranto), had appealed to Pyrrhus, King of Epirus (Map 8) for help. Crossing the Adriatic in 280 BC Pyrrhus defeated the Romans in a hard-fought contest, prompting him to exclaim: 'Another such victory and we are undone', giving rise to the immortal expression, a 'Pyrrhic victory'.

Responding to an appeal from the Greek city of Syracuse, still Pyrrhus crossed over to Sicily in 278 BC and was soon in possession of most of the island, driving the Carthaginians into its western extremity. His high-handedness, however, eventually lost

him the support of the Greek cities he had come to assist and he was forced to withdraw. As he set sail he looked back and prophetically observed: 'What a field we are leaving to the Carthaginians and the Romans to exercise their arms.' His importance for us in trying to understand the relationship between Carthage and Rome is that he seemingly brought them closer together while they faced him as a common enemy. That said, however, Pyrrhus' adventurous excursion could have extended Roman ambitions beyond the confines of the Italian peninsula, and though there is nothing to suggest that this led directly to the Romans seeking further territorial gains, it must have encouraged the patriarchal Claudii family, who favoured a southerly expansion, to oppose the powerful Fabii, whose interests lay to the north, where some 300 of the family had been killed defending the frontiers.

Antique sculpture of Pyrrhus. (Museo della Civilta, Rome/Edimedia, Paris)

People

The Romans who participated in the conquest of the Greek cities witnessed unimagined wealth and luxury, but they were nevertheless still predominantly a rural society. Their intellectual horizons had not been widened by close contact with others who possessed more questioning minds and more sophisticated standards, and the loosening of their strict, simplistic code of behaviour had hardly begun. The Roman *paterfamilias* ruled his family as an autocrat, instilling obedience, loyalty and integrity with a severity approaching the institutionalised training of the Spartan youth.

The result of this upbringing, upheld and fortified by the rigorous demands of public opinion, was that the Romans displayed high standards and set themselves an ideal of virtue based on willpower, self-restraint, a seriousness devoid of frivolity, perseverance and a binding sense of duty to the family, social group or military unit, all established in the hierarchy of state authority. The importance of the individual was subordinated to his corporate responsibilities, and a willingness to sacrifice his own interests or even his life for the good of his group was accepted as the normal standard of personal conduct.

This gave rise to a pragmatic, dour and persistent breed of men, supported by obedient and respectful wives who occupied themselves with the running of their households and the rearing of children. Few would have held doubts about the rectitude of the state's policies and most were deeply conservative, probably not very imaginative, and profoundly superstitious. They were certainly parochial in outlook but bound together by a powerful moral code of reciprocal loyalty. They were hard-working, brave through training, and hardened mentally and physically by the vicissitudes of nature and a life of laborious toil. They made hardy, courageous and disciplined soldiers, whose strength was tempered only by superstition and the usual measure of human failings.

Religion

As the Romans extended their conquests, so they absorbed the religion and culture of the races they had subjected, and in the process, modified their own earlier animistic worship. It was the influence of the Greek cities in southern Italy and later in Sicily which made the greatest impact. By the 3rd century BC the Greek gods and goddesses had been assimilated by the Romans. Greek names were Romanised: Demeter became Ceres; Poseidon and Ares became Neptune and Mars; Zeus and Hera became Jupiter and Juno; and Aphrodite and Hestia became Venus and Vesta, though this renaming did not change their fickle natures and wanton ways.

There was no established church as we know it, with a hierarchy, creed and moral code. Nor was there a single all-powerful god, but rather a multiplicity of deities interfering with and squabbling over their different interests and mortal protégés. To the majority of Romans the mythology that we regard as little more than a collection of fables was, in varying degrees, a portrayal of immortals to whom established rights were due and who had to be propitiated. The fulfilment of these obligations would ensure the safe return of mariners by Neptune or victory in battle by Mars, while Ceres would provide an abundant harvest and Jupiter, rain. Neglect, on the other hand, would lead to abandonment, if not the purposeful infliction of disaster. Nevertheless, there were a few hardy souls like the consul Publius Claudius Pulcher who, before the battle of Drepana off Sicily, lost patience when the sacred chickens would not eat and so provide a favourable omen. He flung the birds overboard with the short-tempered advice: 'If you won't eat, then try drinking instead.' Whether his subsequent disastrous defeat can be ascribed to his irreverence is a matter for conjecture, though the gods cannot have been too enraged since he managed to escape with his life.

As there was no church, responsibility for official religious ceremonies was a function of the state, the chief officials being the College of Pontiffs, headed by the Pontifex Maximus

Ceres, the Roman goddess of agriculture and corn (Greek Demeter), mother of Persephone. (Ann Ronan Picture Library)

(Chief Priest), who were the judges and arbiters of divine and human affairs and the interpreters of portents, augurs and omens. Their role was of great significance since the gods could only make their wishes known through coded messages. Divination, however, was not confined to these officials; so long as he could afford to do so, no citizen entered into an undertaking of any importance without offering a sacrifice and reading for himself the signs in the victim's entrails.

Beliefs varied considerably, and religion and its role in determining the course of men's lives was as varied as it is now. Even so, after allowing for this individuality, there can be little doubt that religion influenced military decisions. Major ventures were frequently not undertaken through lack of favourable portents, causing delay and hesitancy. Among soldiers too, individual interpretations inevitably had some bearing on the way they faced an impending battle. A favourable omen could raise morale but an unfavourable one could cause anxiety.

Constitution

After the kings had been displaced by consuls, and following a period of strife between the Plebeians (the common people) and the Patricians (the hereditary aristocracy), a more stable and durable constitution evolved. According to Polybius this consisted of three elements: consuls, senators and the people. Each element possessed sovereign powers which were regulated with such scrupulous regard for equality and equilibrium that no one could say for certain whether the constitution was democratic, despotic or aristocratic: the consuls could be regarded as despots, the senators as aristocratic and the people as democratic.

The consuls had complete control of the administration, raising levies on Rome's allies, appointing the military tribunes and spending public money as they chose. They also commanded the legions when the army took to the field. They were, however, only elected for a year, and had to account for their stewardship on leaving office. Moreover, being a pair, they were subject to one another's vetoes. The Senate, which numbered about 300, came to be largely hereditary and aristocratic. It had the right to exercise authority in many public areas without consulting the people, so was also to some extent despotic. The hereditary nature of the Senate inevitably led to the perpetuation of factional party interests, represented by three family clans who exerted a powerful, and at times contradictory, influence on Rome's policy. The Fabii saw Roman and their own interests being best served by a northern expansion, coupled with a policy of moderation and co-operation with Carthage. The Claudii believed that the future of Rome lay to the south and increasingly came to regard Carthage as a rival to be eliminated. Finally, the Aemilii favoured overseas expansion rather more indiscriminately, but later inclined towards the western Mediterranean. The power that remained with the people seems small, but in fact related to a number of important functions. Apart from various assemblies, they also had sole authority for deciding honours, ratifying or refusing peace treaties, passing sentences of death and imposing major fines. The powers to

Neptune, god of the oceans. From an ancient bust.
(Ann Ronan Picture Library)

honour and punish were placed in the hands of the people; in Polybius' view it is these two things and these alone that hold human society together.

As Rome extended her hegemony, states defeated in battle were allied to Rome by treaty and incorporated into the Roman Confederacy. Those with the strongest ties were the Latin cities, amongst which Rome had originally been counted when the Latins had settled around the lower reaches of the River Tiber and named the region Latium. Except for foreign policy, allied states were permitted a considerable measure of local government, were free to retain their political parties and they paid no tribute.

Though Roman garrisons were established at strategic points, after the 4th century BC the land belonging to the allied states was seldom encroached upon. They were, however, expected to provide troops organised on Roman lines and grouped alongside a Roman legion to form a consular army. The allies did not have to pay for their soldiers' food and weapons, and when called upon to provide troops in excess of their treaty obligations, they received special payments from Rome. In this way Rome was able to field a substantially greater number of men than her limited manpower would have allowed.

The goddess Venus, portrayed on a Roman mosaic from Low Ham, Somerset. (Edimedia, Paris)

Carthaginian and Roman forces on land and sea

The Carthaginian army

Carthage was primarily a trading nation seeking to extend its commercial connections, its sphere of influence and its empire. A maritime nation supported by military force, Carthage was able to maintain her role and trading monopolies for three centuries, mainly through a superior navy which was not averse to sinking rival trade vessels. Such incidents were not regarded as acts of war, especially since many such losses were probably attributed to natural disasters, given the absence of any survivors to testify to the contrary.

The Carthaginian army consisted mainly of mercenaries recruited from the various subject territories who, except in Spain, seldom served in their own countries, and remained isolated from one another through differences of language and religion. They were then largely dependent upon the Carthaginian fleet for supplies, and discipline was enforced via a strict code which included capital punishment. Each territory provided special military skills: Numidia supplied a nimble, courageous and indefatigable cavalry armed with spears and javelins. These lightly clad horsemen, who rode without saddle or bridle, had superb fighting skills, both in the hills or on the plains, manoeuvring like flocks of starlings that wheel and change direction as though by instinct. Threatening and enticing, surprising with sudden and unexpected moves, there was no cavalry on the battlefield to match them.

From the Balearic Islands came the formidable slingers, organised into corps of 2,000 men who were armed with two types of slings, one for long-range engagements against a densely packed enemy and the other for close-quarter, individual targets up to some 600 feet. Their delivery of stones or lead, which could penetrate a helmet or light protective armour, matched the rate of fire and accuracy of contemporary archers. They were savage fighters who were often paid in women rather than gold or silver.

Though infantry soldiers were recruited from Spanish hill tribes, they were in perpetual conflict with one another, a national disharmony which had simplified the Carthaginian conquest of Spain. They were experts at guerrilla warfare but of temperamental disposition and doubtful loyalty, not best suited to set-piece battles. Their basic weapon was a short sword suitable for cutting and thrusting. Also recruited from Spain were lightly armed cavalry whose horses could carry a second rider, ready to dismount and fight as an infantryman.

The largest mercenary contingent, however, were the Libyans of Tunisia. Hardened by the harsh conditions of their own country, they were versatile fighters who served both as light infantry skirmishers and in the heavily concentrated infantry of the line. There were Gauls too but relatively few until Hannibal's invasion of Italy encouraged them to join in substantial numbers to fight their traditional enemies, the Romans. They fought without armour and showed great dash in the attack, but they were unreliable, especially when hard-pressed.

Then there were the elephants. Initially the Carthaginians only used the African elephant found in the forests around Carthage, at the foot of the Atlas mountains and along the coast of Morocco, but later it seems probable that Hannibal obtained some of the larger Indian elephants from Egypt. Until tactics had been developed to counter them on the battlefield, elephants struck terror into men and horses alike and their small numbers were disproportionately

A Numidian cavalryman as shown in an eighteenth-century representation. (AKG, Berlin)

cowardice, as well as bloody mutiny, such incidents were not exclusive to mercenaries. On balance, except for the long time it took to recruit, train and deploy a large mercenary army in an emergency, the defects and inadequacies of the system look exaggerated. The old British Indian Army, with its Sikhs, Gurkhas, Rajputs and Bengalis – to name but a few – incorporating both Hindus and Moslems, was a mercenary army cemented together by its British officers. Whatever the composition of Hannibal's army and however few Carthaginian officers he may have had in relation to his men, these were not factors of great significance; what counted was the magnetism of his leadership.

effective. When frightened, however, they sometimes wreaked devastation in their own ranks by turning and fleeing.

There were also native Carthaginians in the army, but their number was never very great and they were mainly confined to a few hundred heavy infantry called the Sacred Band. From this force the long-term professional leadership was selected, thus ensuring that the generals who commanded the mercenary army came from amongst their own citizens, though the Numidian cavalry did produce their own commanders. Carthage's reliance on a mercenary army was probably caused by the shortage of manpower: there may have been just too few men to do any more than crew their extensive fleet of warships and numerous trading vessels without endangering their commercial activities.

Historians differ in their views as to the effectiveness of the Carthaginian army. Some claim that the mercenaries were not united by any common or reciprocal interest and had no long-term concern for the well-being of those they served, who were, in turn, largely indifferent to the mercenaries anyway. Serving only for money, plunder and rape, they could not be relied upon to face extremes of danger with zeal, or disaster with resolution. Others point out that though there were incidents of desertion and

The Carthaginian navy

The navy played a vital part in the Carthaginian war machine and, unlike the army, it was manned entirely by Carthaginians. There were three basic types of ships: large cargo vessels which were easily converted to troop transports; warships; and small, general-purpose vessels. The cargo vessels, or transports, had rounded hulls to provide capacious holds and were about four times as long as their width. The warships, needing speed rather than capacity, were long and narrow in order to accommodate the greatest possible number of oarsmen. Unlike the earlier Phoenician and Greek triremes which had three levels of oars, each with a single rower, from the 4th century the Carthaginian trireme, and then the quinquereme – the classic warship of the Punic Wars – had four and five rowers respectively, sitting on the same bench and plying the same oar. Thus the sides of the ships were lower than the Greek triremes, which enhanced stability.

Both the trireme and the quinquereme were about 40 metres long and 6 metres wide, with a draught of no more than 2 metres. With 30 oars on each side, they had crews of around 240 and 300 respectively, together with some 30 to 40 sailors who handled the sails and worked on deck. The ships had two

Representing the battle of Lake Trasimene in 217 BC, this painting shows the use of
war elephants. Atributed to Leonard Thiry. (Edimedia, Paris)

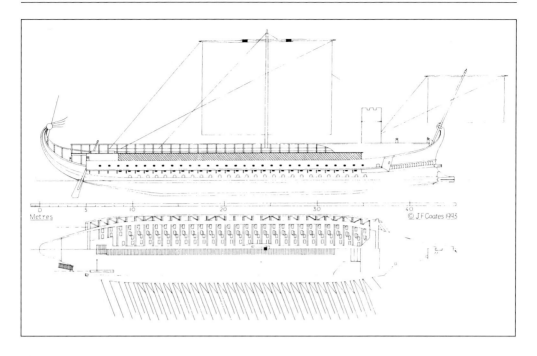

The Carthaginian quinquereme was the work horse of the Punic Wars. No images are extant, but the picture shows a diagram of the Roman quinquereme, based on the relief from the Isola Tiberina monument. (JF Coates)

sets of sails: the central main mast provided propulsion and the smaller mast, mounted on the prow, allowed the ship to be manoeuvred in cross winds. Only sails were used on the approach to a battle area, but once the enemy was sighted, the masts were lowered and the rowers took over. The basic tactical unit consisted of 12 ships, which could be grouped together to form a fleet of varying size – 120 ships, or 10 tactical units, was the normal number.

The general-purpose vessels were smaller, swift and easily manoeuvrable, and were mainly employed on reconnaissance and communication tasks. Two such vessels have been found off the western coast of Sicily and show how the Phoenicians constructed their ships. The wooden components were prefabricated and assembled later. This discovery helps explain how the Romans were able to dismantle and copy a Carthaginian ship once they had captured one. Battles usually took place near the shore, where the ships could be handled in relatively calm water.

There were two basic battle tactics. In both instances the fleet was initially deployed in line ahead, but the subsequent action depended on the enemy's dispositions. If there was sufficient space, the Carthaginian ships would move alongside the enemy and by suddenly turning, ram them amidships. If there was not enough room for this manoeuvre then the Carthaginian vessels would break through gaps in the enemy line and turn about sharply to take them in the rear. The Carthaginians, then, had a potent navy which assured them of sea supremacy at the outbreak of hostilities. With the versatile use of cargo ships as troop transports, they possessed a strategic mobility that offered a unique advantage over any opponent, so long as they had commanders capable of exploiting this superiority.

The Roman army

Under normal conditions all males between the ages of 18 and 46 who satisfied the property criteria were eligible for military service and were recruited into the cavalry or the infantry. The infantry, who were by far the most important arm and formed the main element of the principal fighting formation – the legion – were expected to serve for 20 years. Selection for the cavalry was even more heavily dependent upon wealth, but carried a commitment of just two years. Military service was regarded as a mark of honour without which public recognition and advancement were virtually impossible, especially since it was only after 10 years' duty that a man could hold public office.

A legion consisted of some 4,000 infantry, except in times of special danger when the number was increased to 5,000. These were organised into 10 cohorts, and 300 cavalry who were formed into 10 squadrons. The legion had been developed from the Greek phalanx into a more flexible formation, better able to manoeuvre over broken ground and face the highly mobile Gauls. Each cohort was organised into three *maniples* comprising soldiers of different ages. Forming the first rank were the *hastati*, 120 young men in 12 well spaced files, each 10 men deep; behind the *hastati*, at a distance equivalent to the frontage of the *maniple*, came the *princeps* of 120 slightly older men, again organised into 12 files

10 men deep, so disposed that they faced the gaps between the files of the *hastati* to form a chequerboard pattern. In this way a solid front could quickly be established by either the *hastati* withdrawing or the *principes* advancing. When adopting this more compact order, a legionary standing to arms occupied three feet and, unlike the Greek phalanx, three further feet separated him from the men on either side, thus enabling him to use his sword freely and change the position of his shield. The third *maniple* of 60 older men, usually veterans, were called the *triari*. They were also deployed to cover the gap of those in front of them, but were in six files, each 10 men deep. In addition, each cohort had a squadron of cavalry and 120 light infantry for use as skirmishers, flank protection or to form a rearguard.

The *hastati* in the leading *maniple* were each equipped with a short cutting and thrusting sword, together with two javelins to be thrown on approaching the enemy. The shields they carried were some four feet long and two and a half feet wide, bound

Trireme. (Roger-Viollet)

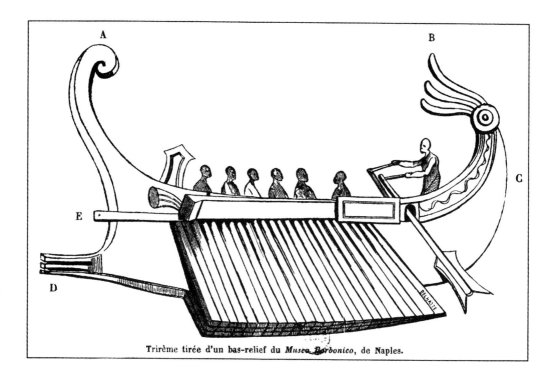

Trirème tirée d'un bas-relief du *Museo Borbonico*, de Naples.

A Balearic slinger. (Osprey Publishing)

with iron at the upper edge to withstand a sword blow and at the bottom to enable them to be rested on the ground without damage. The legionaries wore body armour and helmets, but though the *principes* and *triari* were similarly protected, they carried a spear instead of two javelins. The light infantry were armed with a spear for thrusting or throwing, a sword, and a round shield three feet in diameter. The cavalry, who were not considered much more than an adjunct to the infantry, were poorly armed and wore no body armour.

Command was exercised at four different levels: centurions, tribunes, legates and consuls. The centurions were long-service professional officers equating to company commanders. Two of them were selected by merit to command each maniple, the one on the right being the senior. The cohorts were commanded by tribunes who had either been promoted from amongst the centurions, in which case they would have been battle-hardened professionals, or were magistrates

who had been posted to the army to serve for a few years before returning to civilian life. A legion, which in modern terms could be compared with a division, was commanded by a legate, another temporary civilian appointment, but one of senatorial rank. An army was formed by combining two legions and was commanded by a consul appointed by the Senate. One of the legions was invariably Roman, but as mentioned above, the other was generally recruited from one of the allied cities.

The slow progress that had been made towards improving tactical flexibility was discarded at the battle of Cannae with disastrous consequences. The Romans reverted to massing as a phalanx, in the belief that they would then burst through the thinly drawn Carthaginian centre. Though there were deserters – 900 in Carthage when the city fell – who preferred to fight to the death rather than be taken alive and crucified, we do not know whether they were Roman or mainly from amongst the allies. The legionaries, both Roman and allied, were motivated through a combination of harsh discipline and public esteem. The certain and severe punishment they faced for cowardice was more feared than the prospect of death on the battlefield. Bravery and victory, on the other hand, brought rewards: a triumph for the consul, spoil and esteem for those who had shared in his achievements. The Romans do not appear to have been any braver than their opponents; if they showed greater perseverance over a longer period, it was because of their training and their social conditioning.

The Roman navy

The history of the Roman navy is strange indeed. Following the third treaty between Rome and Carthage, drawn up in 279 BC at the time of Pyrrhus' campaign in Italy, Carthaginian naval supremacy had been recognised: they would aid the Romans by sea should the need arise. The Roman conquest of southern Italy had been achieved with just an army and no attempt had been made to reduce the coastal cities using a combined land and sea assault, or even a blockade. Eventually, however, the Romans recognised their maritime deficiency and with their usual thoroughness set about putting things right. A Carthaginian quinquereme which had run aground during a naval brush was dismantled and used as a model for the construction of a whole Roman fleet.

The recorded facts relate how 100 quinqueremes and 20 triremes were ordered to be ready in two months. While the workmen were busy building and fitting out the ships, the recruiting and training of the sailors proceeded apace. Skeleton ship frames were constructed along the shore and the rowers drilled under the command of their officers. It was a stupendous undertaking involving some 35,000 men, suggesting a considerable amount of pre-planning, with the crews being recruited, the timber felled and shaped, the skeleton frames constructed and the ships themselves all completed before the two months training, including a period at sea, actually began. Even so, it is small wonder that in the first encounters with the Carthaginians the Romans proved to be hopelessly inadequate.

To compensate for their lack of nautical expertise, however, the Romans introduced a technical innovation that exploited their legionaries' aptitude for close-quarter fighting. A 12-foot pillar of wood with a pulley on the top was fitted to the prow of every vessel. To this pillar a boarding bridge was attached which could be hoisted up and swung around in the required direction. At the end of the bridge there was a large pointed spike called a *corvus* which, when released, drove itself into the deck of the opposing vessel, locking the two ships together. Then the legionaries could storm aboard and slaughter the near-defenceless crews. As an example of a technical innovation which led to a precipitous reversal of battlefield superiority that had endured for centuries, the *corvus* outclassed all subsequent developments such as gunpowder, the tank, radar, submarines, air power and electronic warfare.

A Roman sword (*gladius*). (Edimedia, Paris)

Bronze relief of Roman legionaries (Edimedia, Paris)

Collapse of the Third Treaty of Friendship

The causes of war are seldom explicit or simple, nor do they lend themselves to broad generalisations, such as commercial rivalry, social unrest, or religious fanaticism. To isolate one single factor, however prominent, risks over-simplification; equally, to follow too many threads can result in confusion. Furthermore, to rely on subsequent statements by those directly involved is notoriously dangerous: memories of complex events become clouded and perhaps even adjusted, if only subconsciously, with hindsight.

When considering what occurred over 2,000 years ago, it must be recognised that much of the available evidence is fragmentary and, even at the time, the opinions expressed are largely hearsay. Even so, although there may never be any way of determining exactly why Carthage and Rome went to war, there are two clearly identifiable factors which make such a war more probable. First, the Romans saw an opportunity to advantage themselves; secondly they saw that the Carthaginians were unprepared militarily, and succumbed to this temptation. Nothing has changed in human nature during the last 20 centuries. Whether as individuals or collectively, most of the human race displays an unfortunate proclivity for opportunism, unless deterred by the threat of sufficiently painful consequences. Bearing in mind the limitations of this examination, let us then take a look at what occurred.

While the Romans had remorselessly extended their conquests down the length of the Italian peninsula, the Carthaginians had maintained their policy of non-intervention. Whether this was primarily because they were already occupied in Sicily and had no wish to enter a new and potentially hazardous undertaking or whether they felt their overall interests were best secured by not antagonising this emerging power, is not known. But the result remains the same: the Carthaginians did not provoke the Romans any more than the land-bound Romans directly challenged Carthaginian interests. Both powers then appeared to be respecting the Third Treaty of Friendship, drawn up in 279 BC, which amongst other things had committed them to go to one another's assistance if attacked. We have seen how, only a year or two after the treaty, Rome and Carthage were drawn closer together when Pyrrhus first crossed the Adriatic to help the Greek cities opposing Roman domination, then sailed the straits of Messina to assist the Greek cities in Sicily against the Carthaginians. Yet some 10 years later Carthage and Rome were at war: what went wrong?

A modern strategist might point out that the possession of Sicily would have brought untold advantages: strategically placed between Italy and Africa, it provided an important springboard for military operations in either direction, while dominating east–west trade routes across the Mediterranean at its narrowest point. For the Romans it also offered a forward operating base from which sea communications between Carthage, Sardinia and Spain could be interdicted. Yet clearly such an analysis played no part in Roman thinking, since Rome lacked a fleet for its implementation. That the Carthaginians could have pursued such reasoning is more plausible, but they had shown no wish to renew their earlier endeavours to conquer Sicily so their goal seems to have been limited to achieving a monopoly of trade throughout the island.

Bronze coin of the Mamertini. (The British Museum)

There are two other considerations which support this contention. Spain was by far the most important source of wealth for the Carthaginians, and their attention must have been drawn westwards rather than towards an area in which they had had so much difficulty in establishing a presence. Secondly, whenever the Carthaginians had mounted an expedition to Sicily, it had been in response to the loss of their trading possessions, not in direct search of further conquests. As there was no such expeditionary force in Sicily during the period we are considering, it can be concluded that the Carthaginian state of readiness was far too low to undertake a major campaign. We must, then, look for less dynamic reasons for war.

The straits of Messina. (Roger-Viollet)

First hostilities

The actual catalyst for conflict was a request
by some unscrupulous adventurers called
the Mamertines, from Campania on the
western seaboard of the Italian peninsula.
The Mamertines had fought in Sicily as
mercenaries for Agathocles of Syracuse
against the Carthaginians. After Agathocles'
death in 289 BC the inhabitants of
Messana welcomed the Mamertines into
their city and the Mamertines promptly
set about massacring the leading citizens,
appropriating their wives and property, and
creating a vassal empire around the city
which extended over the north-east corner
of the island. This brought them into
conflict with Hiero of Syracuse, who was
building an empire to succeed that of
Agathocles. Adopting a high moral tone,
Hiero condemned the Mamertines for the
treacherous manner by which they had
obtained Messana 15 years earlier and,
marching north with his army, he brought
them to battle on the Longanus river, where
he defeated them decisively.

Before Hiero could reap the full rewards
of this victory, however, the Carthaginians
moved swiftly to assist the Mamertines by
placing a garrison in Messana. This prompt
action did not arise from any concern for
the Mamertines but rather from a
determination that the Syracusans, against
whom the Carthaginians had waged war for
so many years, should not obtain possession
of the harbour of Messana and so be in a
position to dominate the narrow straits
between Sicily and Italy.

Although they had been saved from Hiero,
who quickly realised that he was no match for
the Carthaginians and withdrew to Syracuse,
the Mamertines had no wish to be subjected
to a regime that put the orderly conduct of
trade before their own self-interested piracy.
Furthermore, since the Carthaginians had not
displayed great consistency of purpose or
undisputed skill in their military campaigns,
the wheel of fortune might take a less
favourable turn and leave the city once again
exposed to the ambitions of Hiero. An

alliance with the Romans looked a better
bet: they were after all fellow countrymen
with a shared heritage; furthermore, the
Romans allowed a considerable degree of
independence to the cities and tribes they
had assimilated into their Confederation.
Envoys were despatched to Rome, seeking
an alliance and Roman protection.

This request put the Romans on the
horns of a dilemma. Agreeing to it would
clearly risk war with Carthage; not doing
so would mean letting an opportunity to
secure a foothold in Sicily slip away. The
move was strongly advocated by those like
the Claudii who believed that the future of
Rome lay in the south.

The Senate was probably divided, on
account of its changing social composition.
The old families who had once dominated
the Senate by aristocratic right were seeing
their position eroded by the promotion of a
new class of men who had either won
distinction on the battlefield or recognition
in the democratic assembly of the people.
Another war would threaten the Senate
with a renewed influx of candidates borne
on a wave of public fervour. Additionally,
the popular assembly had acquired
increasing influence and power because
of its ultimate right to declare war and
approve terms of peace, while the Senate
was still left responsible for the direction
of the war and the consequences of failure.
The people had thus acquired power
without responsibility; the Senate was
attempting to combine in a single assembly
two diverse factions, one based on the
inherited privilege of aristocratic birth and
the other on plebeian approval.

Apart from these conflicting interests, in
which the views of the Claudii prevailed,
there were obvious attractions in responding
positively to the Mamertines' appeal. As
long as the Carthaginians held Messana they
were in a position to dominate the Straits
with their all-powerful fleet and, more
menacingly, they might be tempted to
extend their conquests on to the mainland
of Italy. Thus the occupation of Messana by
a Roman garrison would not only provide a

foothold for further expansion, but also ensure that the key cities either side of the Straits were in Roman hands. No doubt there were some who also saw an opportunity to secure the whole of Sicily as a Roman province, but the inherent dangers of such a position probably deterred all but the most ardent.

There must have been much debate about the recently reaffirmed treaty with Carthage which declared friendship and a readiness for military co-operation; any unprovoked breach of this treaty would be seen as an act of flagrant aggression. The argument that the despatch of Roman troops would only be in response to an appeal for protection against Syracuse and not directed against Carthage was sheer sophistry: a Carthaginian garrison was already installed and would have to be evicted. For Rome to be perceived as an aggressor would not only be a contradiction of the virtuous standards so purposefully inculcated into her people, but would also endanger her dealings with the other states which were, at least in public relations terms, based on equally noble ideals.

There was a further moral problem facing those in the Senate who pressed for the occupation of Messana. A few years earlier the Roman garrison in Rhegium had seized control of the city and established a tyrannical government similar to the one which the Mamertines, probably in imitation, now practised. When Rhegium was eventually recaptured the mutinous survivors were assembled in the Forum in Rome, flogged and then beheaded. What then was the moral justification in responding to a call for assistance from criminals in Messana who had been fortunate in preserving their skins, if not their possessions, under Carthaginian protection? The answer was self-evidently none.

At the time of the Mamertine request, there was nothing to suggest that the Romans had anything to fear from the Carthaginians in the foreseeable future. In Messana itself there was only a small garrison, and the hesitancy of its commander, Hanno, in resisting the Romans when they did eventually land, which in his crucifixion, hardly suggests that he or his troops were preparing for a Carthaginian invasion of Italy. Even the Carthaginian fleet was absent from the harbour of Messana and had done nothing to contravene the Third Treaty of Friendship, let alone attempt to dominate the Straits. Surprisingly, however, although lacking both provocation and a fleet to transport and sustain their army, the Senate could not persuade its contesting factions to determine a rational policy, and instead delegated the responsibility for reaching a decision to the popular assembly.

Though constitutionally correct, this was a high-risk enterprise relying as it did on a popular vote that was probably even more heavily influenced by powerful voices with vested interests than would have been the Senate itself. This does not mean that Rome and Carthage would not have eventually fought for supremacy in the Mediterranean – given Rome's imperialistic ambitions and Carthaginian preoccupation with their commercial empire this was almost inevitable – but in 264 BC there was no obvious reason for these two powers to become embroiled in a major war. The fact that they did so, and over such a minor and unworthy cause, was unequivocally the fault of the Romans.

When commenting on the Punic Wars, reference to the three levels of war – strategic, operational and tactical – helps explain the course of the fighting. This is not to suggest that either Carthage or Rome possessed such a military vocabulary or indeed recognised the conceptual differences between these three levels.

Strategic level: the definition of strategic objectives to be achieved in fulfilment of government policy.

Operational level: the planning and execution of military operations to achieve stated strategic objectives.

Tactical level: the planning and conduct of battles in pursuit of the operational aim.

To put it simply, having decided what you want to do, you plan how this is to be achieved and co-ordinate the actual battles to be fought in its fulfilment.

The three Punic Wars

The First Punic War 264–241 BC

For the sake of clarity, the First Punic War will be considered in four phases, though the fighting in Sicily did not end in 261 BC and then begin again three years later. Something of a stalemate had been reached, so the Romans shifted the war's centre of gravity to North Africa, leaving Sicily very much a backwater. Similarly, the war at sea did not end in 256 BC, but thereafter it formed such an integrated part of the land campaign that they are best considered together. The four phases are:

The opening round in Sicily	264–261 BC
The maritime dimension	260–256 BC
The African campaign	256–255 BC
The return to Sicily	254–241 BC

The opening round in Sicily 264–261 BC

After the decision had been taken to aid the Mamertines, the problem facing Appius Claudius, the commander of the expedition, was that his two legions were some 400 miles north of their port of embarkation at Rhegium and the necessary shipping, all of which belonged to the allies, had to be assembled. Appreciating that any delay would cost him the element of surprise, Claudius despatched a smaller force, which managed to cross the Straits undetected and quickly secure the town of Messana, allowing the Carthaginian garrison to leave unmolested. However, Hanno, the unfortunate Carthaginian commander, was subsequently crucified for his lack of resolution.

Appius Claudius was later able to make a night crossing with his main force without being intercepted, though he must have been detected as it was then that the Carthaginian quinquereme, which served as

the model for the construction of a Roman fleet, charged so furiously that it ran aground. Once ashore, Claudius found himself confronted by the Carthaginians under Hanno and the Syracusans under Hiero. These two former opponents failed to co-ordinate, let alone concentrate, their respective forces, so were defeated separately, though not decisively. Both were able to withdraw, Hanno into some neighbouring Carthaginian cities and Hiero into Syracuse, which became the Romans' next objective.

With two new consuls and reinforced by a further two legions, the Romans' determination and overwhelming force quickly persuaded 67 Syracusan and Punic cities to reach an accommodation with Rome; shortly afterwards Hiero too entered into an alliance.

Meanwhile the Carthaginians had been raising a mercenary army, mainly from Spain, and when their training had been completed they were transported to the fortified city of Agrigentum on Sicily's south coast. Here the Carthaginians were besieged but managed to slip out through the Roman lines during the night, leaving the hapless population to be butchered. Until the capture of Agrigentum, the Romans had drawn a distinction between the garrisons of foreign cities and the civilian population, but with the ferocious reprisals that had now been taken, an example was set which possibly was intended to serve as a warning to others contemplating siding with Carthage. The effects of this new policy are not clear; some inland cities went over to the Romans, but those on the coast which could be sustained by the Carthaginian fleet stood firm.

Whatever the members of the Claudii had hoped for, with their ambitions for southern expansion, there was no long-term Roman strategic objective for becoming involved in

Eighteenth-century copperplate engraving of a Roman warship, showing the *corvus*, the beam with which the Romans attacked other ships. (Ann Ronan Picture Library)

Sicily; more an uncertain drift towards total conquest. On the other hand, for the first three years of the war the field commanders were quite clear as to their operational objectives: the occupation of Messana, the subjugation of Syracuse and the reduction of Agrigentum. These precise aims had enabled them to achieve a concentration of force and to take and hold the offensive.

In 261 BC, however, the situation was reversed. There was now an unequivocal strategic objective to clear the Carthaginians from Sicily but no operational plan as to how this was to be achieved. Roman strength lay in the set-piece battle, the decisive clash of opposing armies that settled the issue one way or another, but Hamilcar, the Carthaginian commander who had replaced Hanno, was not to be drawn. Instead he used the flexibility within his fleet to dominate the seaboard and its cities. The fighting then became diffuse and

reactive as city after city flared into revolt or declared for Carthage. The problem facing the Romans was that even if they were to seek a conclusive action by first concentrating against the main Carthaginian base at Lilybaeum on the west coast, they would be unable to reduce it by siege unless they were able to prevent reinforcements and provisions coming in by sea. Meanwhile, they would incur the risk of being cut off from their own supplies, as had nearly occurred at Agrigentum. An entirely land-based strategy could not break this stalemate and the need for a Roman fleet was self-evident.

The maritime dimension 260–256 BC

We have seen how the Romans hastily constructed a fleet, and to compensate for their inferior seamanship raised *corvi* on the prows of their ships to enable the legionaries to swarm aboard opponents' vessels. It was

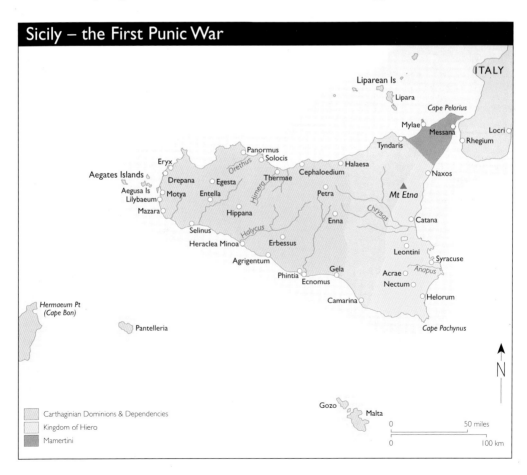

Sicily – the First Punic War

Carthaginian Dominions & Dependencies
Kingdom of Hiero
Mamertini

0   50 miles

0   100 km

in 260 BC at Mylae (Milazzo), on the north coast near Messana, that this development was first used, when 130 Carthaginian ships closed with a superior Roman fleet of 145 vessels and lost nearly half their total strength in the encounter. The victory at Mylae presented the Romans with two strategic options: either they could continue the Sicilian campaign, or they could go on to the defensive in Sicily and assault the African mainland with a view to destroying Carthage. They decided on the former, maintaining a consistent strategic objective but one which required a change of operational tactics.

Though the Romans had energetically sought to enlarge their fleet, like their army, it was still not sufficiently powerful to deal with widely spread objectives. Yet in 258 BC, this is exactly what they attempted to do: instead of concentrating their resources and mounting

Relief showing a Roman trireme with legionaries on board. (Sopraintendenza Archeologica per le Provincie di Napoli e Caserta)

combined land and sea operations against the coastal cities in Sicily, so cutting their supply lines to Carthage, or alternatively, ending the politically embarrassing raids against the Italian seaboard by subjugating Sardinia and Corsica, the Romans attempted to conduct both campaigns at once. The result was that, although the Romans won another naval victory and had some successes in Corsica, they were too weak to exploit their achievements and in Sicily they suffered a severe reverse when Hamilcar Barca suddenly took the offensive. The prevailing stalemate led to growing disenchantment and then to an alternative strategy: to carry the war to North Africa. In so doing they set the scene for one of the largest naval battles in history.

In the summer of 256 BC a Roman fleet of 330 ships, of which 250 were probably quinqueremes, set sail southward from Messana, along the eastern coast of Sicily to Phintias, a substantial port on the southern coast lying under Mt Ecnomus, where two legions were waiting to embark. Meanwhile the Carthaginian fleet, which was about the same warship strength, sailed from Lilybaeum, and following the shoreline, encountered the Romans as they set sail for Africa.

The Roman commander, Marcus Atilius Regulus, had divided his fighting ships into four squadrons. Two made up the sides of a triangle, the third, with the transports in tow, formed the base, while the fourth squadron deployed in a single, extended line to the rear to cover the flanks of the third squadron and the transports. The Carthaginians also divided their fleet into four squadrons. Three were placed in line from the shore so that the one on the extreme seaward right did not directly face the Roman wedge but remained free to advance and attack their left flank. The fourth was deployed forward of the others, parallel to the shore, so that it was already in position to attack the Roman right flank without having to change direction.

The Roman wedge drove forward towards the Punic fleet. As they approached the two squadrons directly facing them, the Carthaginians turned and feigned flight. The Romans then hastened in pursuit but in doing so, became separated from the third squadron towing the transports. At a signal from Hamilcar, the Carthaginian commander, the two squadrons pretending to flee turned on their pursuers; the squadron that had been deployed beyond the Roman wedge fell upon its rear, and the squadron posted parallel to the shore advanced to attack the Roman squadron that was towing the transports. Three separate battles raged and the hapless transports were cast off and left to drift unattended. For a while both navies held their own, but eventually, despite their brilliant initial tactics, the Carthaginian squadrons engaging the apex of the Roman

wedge were forced to flee in earnest, leaving the Romans free to turn back and assist their other hard-pressed squadrons. Now heavily outnumbered, the Carthaginians' two remaining squadrons were broken and forced to withdraw as best they could.

Once again the *corvi* had proved their usefulness, and although nearly as many Roman ships were sunk as Carthaginian, 24 and 30 respectively, 64 Carthaginian ships were captured. The Romans were now free to cross over to Africa, but some delay occurred while essential repairs were completed, not only to their own vessels but to the Carthaginian ships, which were now pressed into service. When all was ready the Romans put to sea a second time, while the Carthaginians abandoned any attempt to hold forward in the seas around Sicily but fell back to the Gulf of Carthage. Instead of making the direct approach anticipated by the Carthaginians and sailing into the gulf on the western side of Cape Bon, the Romans made an indirect approach and disembarked on the eastern seaboard, thus accepting the greater natural obstacles on land that would have to be overcome in the march on Carthage rather than risking another sea battle.

The African campaign 256–255 BC

The Carthaginians did not have enough troops in Africa to do more than defend Carthage, so they withdrew into the city leaving the Romans to establish themselves ashore without hindrance some 40 miles along the coast to the east. Though the delay following the battle of Ecnomus may have caused considerable disruption, as messengers had to be sent back to Rome seeking further instructions, it appears that the Romans' operational planning had again been defective. They had probably assessed that Carthage, like the fortified coastal cities of Sicily, could only be taken if blockaded from both land and sea. Winter, however, was now approaching and it would have been too late to undertake such an enterprise. There was also a logistical problem with the fleet: if it were to remain in North Africa the Romans faced the task of feeding some 75,000 rowers, who greatly outnumbered the soldiers. It is hardly surprising then that when orders arrived from Rome, only 40 warships were to remain, with 15,000 infantry and 500 cavalry. The others, including all the transports, were to return to Rome. Loading on board the 20,000 slaves that had been rounded up, together with booty, one consul went on his way leaving the other, Marcus Atilius Regulus, the co-victor of Ecnomus, with two legions and sufficient ships to keep open communications with Rome.

After recalling 5,000 infantry and 500 cavalry from Sicily, the Carthaginians felt strong enough to try to prevent the Romans ranging unopposed through the countryside, plundering at will. Their foray, however, was swiftly defeated and this encouraged the Romans to advance their forward base to Tunis, a few miles south-west of Carthage.

Fame and a triumph now lay within Regulus' grasp; all that was required of him was the reduction of Carthage, apparently tottering on the brink of starvation. This was not, however, to prove so easy. Responding to a Carthaginian appeal to the Greeks, Xanthipus, a Spartan general who had received the rigorous training associated with his countrymen, had arrived at the head of a substantial number of Greek mercenaries and quickly appreciated that it was Carthaginian generalship that was at fault, not the mercenary soldiers. Having put things right, in the spring of 255 BC Xanthipus marched out of the city with some 12,000 infantry, 4,000 cavalry and an unspecified number of elephants. In the ensuing battle the Romans were routed by the elephants, which smashed into the legionaries. Despite heavy losses they fought on manfully until assailed by the Numidian cavalry from the rear. Only 2,000 of the Romans escaped and some 500 prisoners were taken, including Regulus himself.

When news of the defeat reached Rome, plans had to be radically recast. Abandoning all hope of laying siege to Carthage, an expedition would be mounted instead to rescue any survivors. The strategic aim of the war would then revert to the securing of Sicily. In the early summer, 350 Roman ships sailed to the tip of Cape Bon. There they encountered and heavily defeated the Carthaginian fleet, which thereafter made no effort to intervene. The Romans were then free to re-embark their surviving legionaries unmolested in a thoroughly successful operation. However, they foolishly provoked the weather gods by a display of *hubris*. Scorning the pressing advice of the pilots to steer to the west of Sicily to avoid the sudden summer storms which frequently arose off the southern coast, the Romans met with disaster. Off Camarina, towards the south-eastern extremity of the island, the fleet was struck by a savage storm and all but 80 ships were lost, together with their crews and the soldiers they were transporting. Altogether some 100,000 men may have been drowned. A stupendous effort would now be required to replace their losses. Remarkably, the Romans achieved this in seven or eight months. The Carthaginians also had to replace substantial losses, as well as contend with widespread uprisings throughout their African possessions. Punic primacy and overlordship had been challenged. It would have to be re-established before Carthage could confidently resume the struggle.

The return to Sicily 254–241 BC

In the spring of 254 BC the new consuls left Italy with two fresh armies and 220 new ships, bound for Messana. There they joined up with the ships and survivors from the disastrous storm off Camarina. Once preparations had been completed, the 300-strong fleet sailed round Cape Pelorias along the north coast, while the legions marched to Drepana, embarked and then sailed to Panormous (Palermo), one of the largest and richest Carthaginian coastal cities, with a good harbour. The Romans landed under the outer walls that encircled the town, breached these defences and set about butchering its inhabitants, a sight which must have encouraged those sheltering behind the old city's inner defences to surrender and face slavery.

The battle of Ecnomus

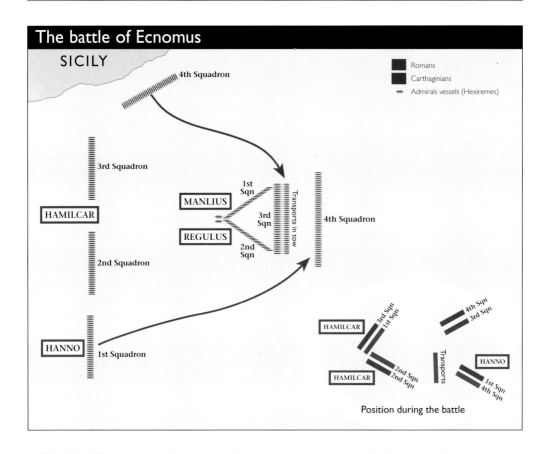

SICILY

4th Squadron

Romans
Carthaginians
Admirals vessels (Hexiremes)

3rd Squadron

HAMILCAR

2nd Squadron

HANNO   1st Squadron

1st Sqn
MANLIUS
3rd Sqn
REGULUS
2nd Sqn

Transports in tow

4th Squadron

3rd Sqn
1st Sqn
HAMILCAR
4th Sqn
3rd Sqn

HAMILCAR
2nd Sqn
2nd Sqn

Transports

HANNO

1st Sqn
4th Sqn

Position during the battle

The fall of Panormous induced a number of other cities to throw in their lot with Rome, leaving the Carthaginians mainly confined to the west of the island. But in 253 BC the Romans lost sight of their strategic objective. The two new consuls travelled through Sicily and crossed over to North Africa, not to threaten Carthage but to raid the Libyan coastline some 200 miles to the south. The Romans probably wished to sustain the unrest among the Libyans, but this division of their resources proved ineffectual. Having been fortunate not to lose their fleet off the Libyan coast when it was ignominiously stranded on an ebb tide, the Romans were caught in a storm on the passage back and lost 150 of their 200 ships.

For the next two years Roman resolution seemed to falter. The land campaign was conducted in a desultory manner and the lost ships were only partially replaced. The Carthaginians on the other hand had quelled

the dissident Libyans and sent reinforcements to Sicily under Hasdrubal, the son of Hanno, who had served with Xanthipus. For two years he dominated the countryside around Lilybaeum, but he was eventually defeated in a messy battle near Panormous from which he managed to escape. He was later recalled to Carthage and, like his father, summarily executed; being a Carthaginian general was no sinecure.

Though the Romans finally received naval reinforcements and troops for the investment of Lilybaeum, they were unable to prevent the garrison being supplied from the sea, while on land they faced a Herculean task. Although they had four legions available, the city lay on a promontory and was secured by a massive wall and a deep ditch that required the erection of siege fortifications. Not long after these had been completed a violent wind blew down some of the Roman towers protecting their works, and this encouraged the Carthaginians to sally forth and set them ablaze. Following this reverse, the Romans gave up trying to take the city by storm and settled down to starve the garrison into submission. Eight years later, when the First Punic War ended, Lilybaeum remained unconquered.

The Romans' next move was to try to destroy the Carthaginian fleet sheltering at Drepana, just north of Lilybaeum. Publius Claudius Pulcher, who had earlier flung the sacred chickens overboard, set sail with 120 ships, none of which were now equipped with the *corvus*, since it adversely affected their handling, especially in bad weather. However, surprise was lost and the Romans found themselves trapped between the shore and the Carthaginian fleet. Unable to manoeuvre and less experienced than the Carthaginian sailors, the Roman fleet was virtually destroyed, though Pulcher managed to escape with about 30 ships. He was fortunate not to be a Carthaginian as, although responsible for the loss of some 20,000 lives, on his return to Rome he suffered no more than public disgrace and a heavy fine.

While these dramatic events had been unfolding, at the other end of the island

Cape Bon. (Bury Peerless)

a massive Roman fleet consisting of 120 warships and 800 transports, had sailed from Messana and, after rounding Cape Pachynus (Cape Passero), found itself facing the Carthaginian fleet. Before any serious fighting could begin, the Carthaginians, recognising the signs of a pending storm, broke off the engagement and took shelter in the lee of the cape, where they were able to ride out the rough weather. The Roman fleet never had a chance to escape, so was driven on to the rocky shore and almost annihilated.

Roman fortunes were at a low ebb but the Carthaginians were not faring much better. Success at sea had been nullified by impotence on land and most importantly, following the ousting of the war party by the great landowners, attention was diverted from Sicily to interests nearer home. On the positive side, Hamilcar Barca, Hannibal's father, a skilful and energetic commander, had been despatched to Sicily, but he had not the resources to do more than conduct a guerrilla war while the Carthaginian fleet was withdrawn. This was as a result of political rivalries. After four years of inconclusive fighting, the Roman Senate decided to make a supreme effort to end the costly and unrewarding conflict. In 243 BC a new fleet was constructed, which set sail the following year to seal off Lilybaeum from the sea.

Only late in the day did the Carthaginians recognise the danger and return to Sicilian waters to confront the Romans in the naval battle that was to decide the war. It was not an engagement marked by audacious manoeuvre: the two fleets lined up and clashed head on to slog it out until, after losing more than 50 ships, the Carthaginians conceded defeat and retired to Carthage.

Deserted and with no hope of further support, Hamilcar Barca was left to negotiate the best peace terms he could with Catulus, the Roman commander. In the event both commanders showed themselves to be reasonable in their demands, and a treaty was concluded whereby the Carthaginians would retain their arms but withdraw from Sicily and pay a substantial war indemnity. After

24 years of fluctuating fortunes, with a heavy cost in lives and resources, the war had ended, but it was not to bring peace to either side.

Strife between wars 241–218 BC

Almost as soon as the treaty between Lutatius Catulus and Hamilcar Barca had been signed, both Carthage and Rome found themselves engaged in bitter fighting against other opponents. For Carthage it was first against her mutinous mercenaries and then the conquering of Spain. For the Romans it was a renewal of the age-old conflict with the Gauls and then an extension of their power across the Adriatic into Illyria. Though these conflicts were not sequential, for clarity's sake they will be related as though this were; when they interacted with the Punic Wars, as they sometimes did, this will be brought out.

The mercenary revolt 241–237 BC

The cause of the revolt by the mercenaries on returning to Carthage from Sicily was twofold: arrears of pay and the unfulfilled promises of special rewards in recompense for all they had faced during the long years of arduous campaigning. Carthaginian prevarication led to an open revolt, headed by two rabble-rousers who had nothing to lose: Spendius, a fugitive Roman slave who feared the prospect of being handed over to the Romans to face certain death by torture, and Matho, an African who, as the chief instigator of the trouble, could expect a similar fate if taken alive.

Joined by a number of African cities that had been subjected to exorbitant taxes and had had land confiscated as the cost of the war had emptied the Carthaginian treasury, the vicious war spread and lasted for three years. Eventually the mercenary army was trapped against an unidentified range of mountains and was destroyed. The cost in lives and material resources had been enormous, out of all proportion to the arrears of salary due the Sicilian veterans.

The Gallic invasion 226–220 BC

Spearheaded by the Fabii, who regarded the Alps as forming Rome's natural northern boundary, the Romans had progressively annexed territory from the Gauls inhabiting their fertile plains surrounding the river Po. With no firm boundaries and tribal rivalries, there had been intermittent warring amongst the Gauls themselves as well as with the encroaching Romans. In 226 BC these flickering conflicts came to a head when the Gauls united against the Romans and assembled an army of some 50,000 foot soldiers and 20,000 cavalry and chariots. It was at this crucial moment that news of the Carthaginian conquests in Spain reached the Romans and, as Polybius relates in measured terms: 'They were seized with no small consternation.' The Romans' dread of the Gauls had not diminished since they had devastated Rome in 390 BC, barely 170 years earlier. Now, faced with another invasion that threatened them more directly than anything that was happening in Spain, they settled for a treaty with the Carthaginians designed to limit their territorial expansion.

The Gauls opened the campaign by striking towards Rome through Etruria, on the west coast, plundering and wasting the countryside as they went. After inflicting heavy casualties on a Roman army closing with them, they decided to return home rather than risk losing the vast quantities of booty they had acquired. Still pressed by the Romans, the Gauls took the easiest route along the coast, with their left flank protected by the sea, only to find their way blocked by a full consular army from Sardinia, which had disembarked ahead of them. Trapped between the two Roman armies and fighting back to back, 40,000 Gauls were killed and 10,000 taken prisoner. The way was now left open for the Romans to advance the following year, cross the Po and carry the war into the Gauls' homeland. After another Roman victory, the Gauls sued for peace but their terms were rejected and the fighting resumed. During the next two years, 221 and 220 BC, Cisalpine Gaul was finally conquered.

The Illyrian expeditions 229–219 BC

The initial Roman involvement with Illyria began as a result of the pirates who, regarding the Adriatic as their undisputed hunting ground, sallied forth from amongst the many islands and deep indentations to plunder and murder at will. There was nothing new in this. Back in the fifth century BC the Athenian phrase 'to sail the Adriatic' was just another way of saying 'to undertake a hazardous journey'. The Romans had at first tolerated their losses, but the incidents had become so numerous that two envoys were despatched to demand an explanation from the autocratic Queen Teuta. According to Polybius, Teuta reacted 'like a true woman with much passion and resentment' and then had the envoys murdered, thus igniting war on another front.

The fighting that followed was with the limited aim of establishing Roman control over the eastern shore of the Straits of Otranto. There was never any question of the Romans wanting to subjugate the whole of Illyria; they merely sought to end Illyrian supremacy in the Adriatic by decisively defeating them in battle. The Romans were assisted by the Illyrian commander Demetrius, who, fearing for his own safety after arousing his queen's wrath, had transferred his allegiance, so enabling the Romans to be welcomed as deliverers in some of the coastal cities. This was 229 BC. To secure their position, the Romans next induced a number of inland cities and tribes to sign treaties of friendship before turning northwards to clear the coastline.

In the spring of the following year the Illyrians sued for peace and accepted the resulting restrictions on the movement of their warships, besides paying a substantial tribute. Eight years later, in 220 BC, seeing the Romans' preoccupation with the Carthaginians in Spain, Demetrius flouted their authority by attacking a neighbouring tribe whose independence had been guaranteed by the Romans. The Roman response was vigorous and devastating. The next year an army descended on the coast of Illyria and swiftly annihilated all opposition,

Carthage and its neighbours

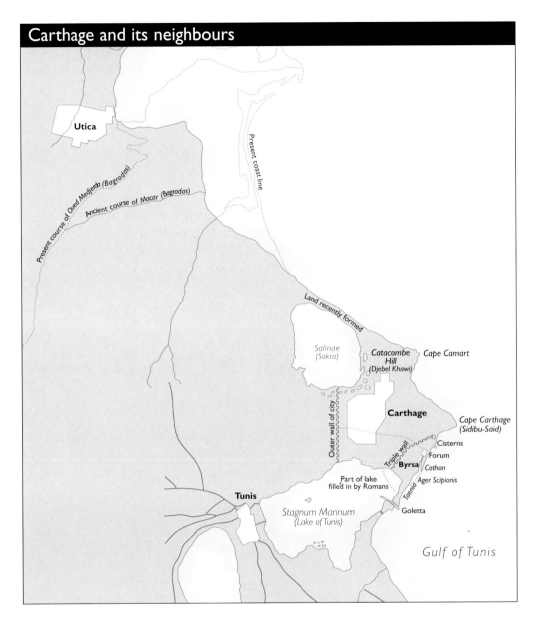

though Demetrius himself escaped to Macedonia, where he assiduously fuelled the latent enmity to Rome. Later this led to Philip of Macedonia entering into an alliance with Hannibal during the Second Punic War.

The conquest of Spain

This is running ahead of events, and we must now step back to 237 BC to see what had been happening in Spain. Having ousted the peace party when the Mercenary War ended, Hamilcar Barca was determined to restore Carthage to her former eminence and avenge the humiliation suffered in Sicily. Appreciating, however, that oligarchic interests could once again prevail and blight his intentions, he decided to establish his own power base and make himself independent of Carthaginian vacillation.

Hamilcar Barca swears an oath of eternal hatred to Rome. Eighteenth-century painting by Claudio Francesco Beaumont. (Edimedia, Paris)

He would conquer Spain and exploit her riches to pay off the war debt and raise a mercenary army whose allegiance was tied to him personally, ultimately enabling him to challenge Rome.

As Carthage no longer had an effective navy, Hamilcar had no alternative but to march along the African coast to the Straits of Gibraltar, with a few supply ships keeping pace with him. In 237 BC he ferried his army across the straits and having done so, proclaimed that he ruled by divine power. This soon transformed simple clan and tribal superstitions into a mystical theology centred on the Barcic family, and a dynastic religion was born that tied the loyalty of the army to him and his relations, while debarring ambitious aspirants from Carthage.

Having established his authority, Hamilcar began his campaign of conquest by securing southern Spain, with its high-quality silver mines, before advancing along the eastern coast. He had hardly achieved these objectives when in 229 BC, while negotiating with a tribal king, he was caught off his guard. In attempting to escape across a swollen river, he was swept from his horse and drowned. He was succeeded by his son-in-law Hasdrubal, who, having ruthlessly avenged Hamilcar's death, extended Carthaginian domination northwards before founding New Carthage, modern-day Cartagena, on the east coast. This gave him possession of a magnificent harbour and further rich silver mines in the surrounding hills. News of these developments reached Rome but, as we have seen, preoccupation with the Gallic invasion meant that the Romans could do little more than draw up a treaty confirming Carthaginian possessions to the south of the Ebro.

In 220 BC Hasdrubal was assassinated in his palace by a Celt whose chieftain had been crucified for plotting against the emperor king. When called upon to elect a successor, the army unanimously voted for the 25-year-old Hannibal, who promptly began to extend Carthaginian territory into the north-western highlands of Spain. When news of these developments reached Rome,

further envoys were despatched who, though convinced that Hannibal was intent upon war, never imagined that this would be fought anywhere but in Spain. Once again Roman attention was focused elsewhere, this time on Illyria, which enabled Hannibal to consolidate his hold on Spain with the capture of the important town of Saguntum after an eight-month siege. Lying some 250 miles north of New Carthage, Saguntum may not have been a formal ally of Rome – the treaty had not as yet been ratified – but as it lay well within the Romans' sphere of influence, its capture and sacking was an irrevocable step towards war.

The Second Punic War 218–201 BC

From the Ebro to the Alps 218 BC
Leaving his brother Hasdrubal Barca in charge of affairs in Spain, in the spring of 218 BC Hannibal set out from New Carthage on a campaign that was to last for 17 years. The plan to march overland had almost certainly been developed by his father, who, having been precipitously abandoned in Sicily as a result of political irresolution and an incompetent fleet, was determined that henceforth he would be master of his own destiny.

After crossing the Ebro, Hannibal was stoutly opposed by tribes who were friendly with Rome and, by the time he had crossed the Pyrenees, his army numbered 50,000 infantry and 5,000 cavalry, with losses of 40,000 and 3,000 respectively since setting out from New Carthage. Not all of these were battle casualties, since a substantial number of Spanish mercenaries had been sent back home (which probably means they deserted). From the Pyrenees to the Rhône, some 160 miles, progress was rapid, since all Hannibal required of the tribes he encountered was freedom of passage and the purchase of provisions. It seems that they were only too willing to help and speed him on his way. On reaching the Rhône, however, Hannibal found the far bank held

Château Queyras, a medieval fortress on the rock referred to by Polybius. (Spectrum Colour Library)

by hostile Gauls, so he delayed his own crossing until a strong detachment had reached the other side further upstream and taken the Gauls in the rear. Using a mass of assorted rafts and canoes, Hannibal's leading troops were able to cross virtually unopposed. After ferrying the rest of the army over, Hannibal headed for the Alps and after reaching the foothills some 10 days later, his long column started threading its way along a narrow pass towards the towering, snow-capped mountains.

After only a few days, the Carthaginians encountered the hostile Allobroge tribe, which had occupied the high ground dominating the pass ahead. Hannibal sent forward a reconnaissance party of Gauls, who reported that the Allobroges abandoned the heights at night, so he ordered them to be seized under cover of darkness and at dawn the advance was resumed. The Allobroges, however, soon found alternative positions and attacked the densely packed column in several places, causing the cavalry horses and pack animals to panic and plunge to their death in the gorge below or turn back to bring chaos to those behind. The situation was only saved by the Carthaginian troops holding the heights attacking the Allobroges from the rear and eventually putting them to flight. For the next five days the army continued its advance unmolested, then encountered another ambush laid by Gauls. Though caught in a deep ravine, after some heavy fighting the Carthaginians forced the Gauls to withdraw and resort to harrying tactics, moving along the mountain ridge to hurl down rocks and stones. However fraught this situation, it was not as desperate as the previous encounter when the Carthaginians had faced a sheer drop on one side.

On the ninth day Hannibal arrived at the main watershed where he rested his men for two days and allowed the stragglers to catch up before starting his descent. Following a steep winding track, made more treacherous by the heavy snow that was now falling, stumbling and sliding, nearly as many men and animals were lost over the precipices as had been killed in the fighting. Their faltering progress was halted by a landslide which blocked the track and had to be cleared. Three days later, 15 days since he had set off to cross the Alps, Hannibal at last reached the fertile expanse of the plains; only 12,000 Africans, 8,000 Spaniards and 6,000 cavalry had survived, about a quarter of the number that had marched out of New Carthage some six months earlier.

The route Hannibal took in crossing the Alps has been convincingly identified by Gavin de Beer in his book *Hannibal* as being the Col de la Traversette. At some 9,000 feet, it is one of the highest passes, accessible through the valley of Queyras with its medieval fortress perched on the top of a huge sugar loaf-shaped rock.

The epic years 218–216 BC

A study of Hannibal's strategy, operational concept and tactical thinking makes it easier to understand the course of his campaign. Although some of the Cisalpine Gauls now joined him, as we have seen, the hard core of his army numbered only 26,000. As for the Romans, we know that at the time of the Gallic invasion, which had flared up only two years previously, the Romans were able to mobilise some 700,000 men. Clearly they could do so again. Though many of these would have been no more than elderly reservists or garrison troops of little military consequence, the Romans still enjoyed a vast numerical superiority, so what was Hannibal's strategic objective? From a treaty drawn up later between Hannibal and Philip V of Macedonia we know that this was not to conquer and subjugate the whole of Italy – an impossible task anyway – but was limited to breaking up the Roman Confederation and reducing it once more to a number of states. These could then be held in check by those whose independence had just been restored to them.

The cohesive power of Rome lay in its army, so Hannibal's operational aim was clearly to inflict such defeats on the army that the subjugated states would be encouraged to rise in revolt. To achieve this, Hannibal would have to avoid being drawn into positional warfare that would permit the Romans to concentrate overwhelmingly against him. This consideration alone debarred Hannibal from tying down his army to some prolonged endeavour such as a city's siege. The fact that he had no siege train was the result and not, as has been suggested, the cause of this restriction. Had he wished to obtain the machines necessary for a siege, he could have arranged for their construction. As it was, he adopted manoeuvre-based tactics to bring the Romans to battle on ground and at a time of his own choosing. Hannibal undoubtedly respected the prowess of the Roman soldier in close combat, but the orderly progression of rigidly linear deployment upon which the Romans relied could be broken using surprise and flexibility – two vital elements of Hannibal's tactical thinking behind which always lay the aim of encirclement.

We will consider Hannibal's campaign in three phases. The first, which is the subject of this section, while only lasting for two years, from 218 to 216 BC, was the most dramatic, when Hannibal's strategic aim of breaking up the Roman Confederation came nearer to fulfilment that at any other time. The second phase, which lasted for four years from 216 to 212 BC, saw Hannibal initially holding the strategic initiative but failing to achieve the encirclement of Italy. The third phase, which lasted 10 years from 212 to 202 BC, saw the consequences of the tide having turned decisively in Rome's favour.

Back in October 218 BC Hannibal rested his army after crossing the Alps, then seized Taurasia (Turin) and defeated Publius Cornelius Scipio and his fellow consul on the

Italy – the Second Punic War

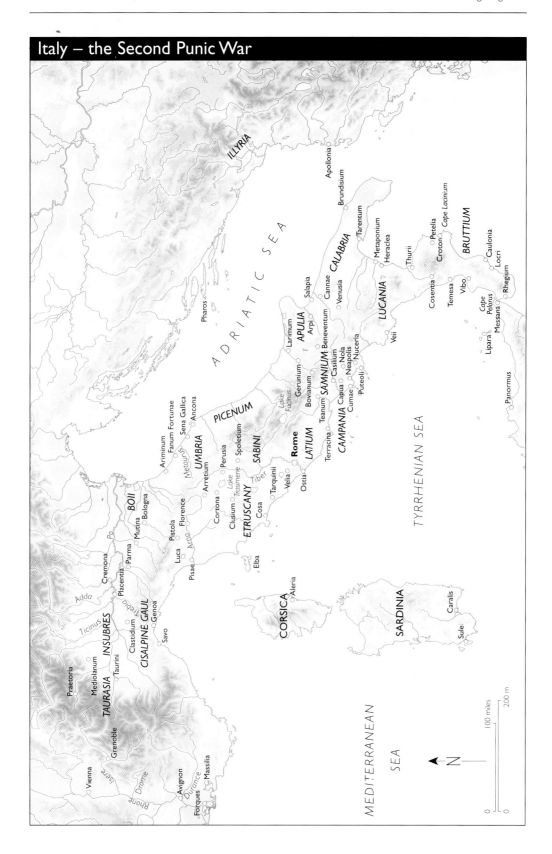

ILLYRIA

Apollonia
Brundisium
CALABRIA
Tarentum
Metaponium
Heraclea
Thurii
Croton
Petelia
Cape Lacinium
BRUTTIUM
Caulonia
Locri
Rhegium
Cosentia
Temesa
Vibo
Cape Pelorus
Messana
Lipara
Panormus

Pharos

A D R I A T I C   S E A

Salapia
Cannae
Venusia
LUCANIA
Veii

Larinum
APULIA
Arpi
SAMNIUM
Beneventum
Casilium
Nola
Neapolis
Nuceria
Puteoli
Cumae
Capua
CAMPANIA
Gerunium
Bovianum
Teanum
Terracina

Lake
Fucinus

PICENUM
Ancona
Sena Gallica
Fanum Fortunae
Ariminum
UMBRIA
Spoletium
Perusia
SABINI
Rome
LATIUM
Tiber
Velia
Ostia

Metaurus
Arretium
Cortona
Clusium
Lake
Trasimene
ETRUSCANY
Tarquinii
Cosa
Elba

BOII
Bologna
Mutina
Parma
Cremona
Placentia
Pistola
Florence
Luca
Arno
Pisae
Genoa
Adda
Ticinus
Trebia
INSUBRES
Clastidium
CISALPINE GAUL
Savo
Praetoria
Mediolanum
Taurini
TAURASIA

Po

Aleria
CORSICA

Caralis
SARDINIA
Sule

TYRRHENIAN SEA

Vienna
Grenoble
Isère
Rhône
Drôme
Durance
Avignon
Forques
Massilia

MEDITERRANEAN
SEA

N

100 miles
200 m
0
0

Tribia, a tributary of the Po. These two deft
and determined successes won over most
of the Cisalpine Gauls, who until then had
been divided in their support for the
Carthaginians. The following spring Hannibal
marched south through Etruria, burning and
devastating the countryside, keeping Cortona
and the hills surrounding it to his left and
making as though to pass Lake Trasimene to
his right. Gaius Flaminius, who had failed
to intercept Hannibal because of his and the
Senate's conviction that Hannibal's objective
was Rome, now set off in pursuit, without
waiting for his fellow consul to join him.
Here we have an example of religious
observances affecting military operations.
Intolerant of any delay, Flaminius had
scorned the usual preliminary sacrifices and
vows on assuming command. Instead he had
taken over in the field, leaving his fellow
consul, Geminus Gnaeus Servilius, to busy
himself with the traditional formalities.

When Hannibal reached Lake Trasimene,
after following the northern shoreline, he set
an ambush along a strip of land between the
defile of Borghetto and Tuoro. Here, facing
the lake, a semicircle of hills forms a natural
amphitheatre. The shore area would have
been considerably smaller than it is today
since the water level was lowered by the
construction of a canal between the lake and
the river Nector in the fifteenth century.
Hannibal positioned his Spanish and Libyan
infantry conspicuously on the ridge to the
west of Tuoro, while the Balearic slingers and
his light infantry concealed themselves on
the high ground facing the lake. Similarly,
the cavalry and Gauls were hidden in folds
in the ground running down to the
Borghetto defile. In this way the entire
area encircled by the hills was dominated
by the Carthaginians.

Flaminius reached Lake Trasimene, near
Borghetto, late in the evening, and at dawn
the legions started to move forward through
the defile across the valley floor. Seeing
Hannibal's troops drawn up in battle to their
front, the Romans deployed into line until
the bulk of the two legions had passed
through the Borghetto defile. Suddenly

assaulted by the light infantry and Balearic
slingers on their left flank and the Numidian
cavalry to their rear, blocked in front and
hemmed in by the lake to their right, most
of the Romans died where they stood. Others
were either weighed down by their armour
and drowned, or were despatched by the
Numidians, who rode out into the lake after
them. Though some 6,000 managed to fight
their way out of the trap, at least 15,000 are
estimated to have died, amongst them the
impious Flaminius. However, the Romans'
woes were not yet over. Servilius, who was
belatedly hurrying down the Via Flaminia,
was intercepted by a mixed force
commanded by Maharbal, the Numidian
cavalry commander, and routed. Half the
men of the two legions were killed and the
remainder taken prisoner.

When the magnitude of the defeat
reached Rome, the city was thrown into a
state of near despair, with the crowds
thronging the public places as the wildest
rumours spread. Thoroughly alarmed, the
Senate appointed an aristocrat, Fabius
Maximus, as dictator with full *imperium*,
which meant that, unlike the consuls, he did
not have to consult the Senate about his
plans. At the head of four legions Fabius
marched down the Via Appia and closed up
to Hannibal, but he had no intention of
accepting battle in circumstances of
Hannibal's choosing. Instead he would
hover, threatening and harrying Hannibal
but keeping to the high ground to nullify
the superiority of the Numidian cavalry in
particular. He earned himself the title
Cunctator, or 'The Delayer'. This was a
difficult course to pursue, not least because it
left Hannibal free to burn and plunder at
will while the Romans looked on, apparently
too timid to intervene. Such a policy could
not endure. The allies could not be expected
to remain loyal under such circumstances
and internal political pressures for resolute
action were too strong. At the end of Fabius'
year as dictator he was replaced, in 216 BC,

Saguntum, captured by Hannibal. The gate theatre is a
later Roman addition. (Roger-Viollet)

The battle of Lake Trasimene

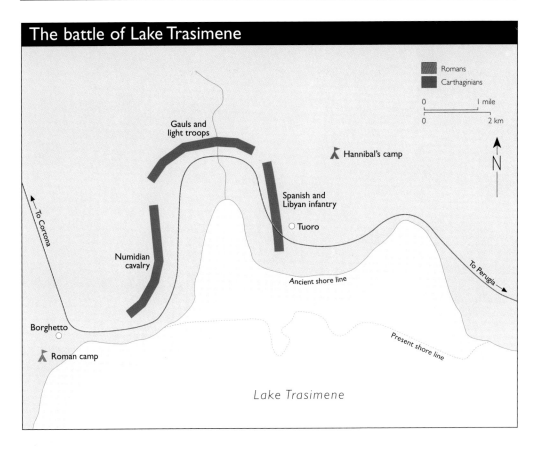

by two consuls, Marcus Terentius Varro and
Lucius Aemilius Paulus.

The Senate decided that Hannibal must
be brought to battle, so four new legions
were mobilised and ordered to join the four
already shadowing Hannibal in Apulia;
concentrated together they would then
crush him, in accordance with traditional
military thinking. So it was that the fatal
day arrived and it was Varro who exercised
command at Cannae when, at first light, he
moved the Roman army across the river
Aufidus on to the east bank. He positioned
the cavalry on the right wing, resting on the
river, with the legions next to them and the
cavalry of the allies on the left wing. In
front of the whole army were the light
infantry. The deployment was conventional
enough, but Varro shortened the frontages
of the legions and reduced the distances
between the *maniples* within them. There
was a reversion to the theory of sheer mass,
so flexibility was renounced and the rigidity

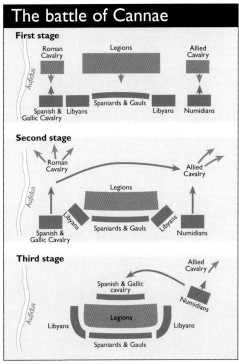

View of Lake Trasimene, looking down from where the
Gauls and light horse were. The cavalry were behind the
hill on the right of the picture, beyond which lies the defile
of Berghetto, on the lake's shore. (Author's collection)

of the phalanx was reinstated. The Roman
army numbered some 80,000 infantry and
more than 6,000 cavalry.

While the Romans were completing their
deployment, Hannibal brought his army into
line. His light infantry and Balearic slingers
formed a screen behind which his main force
matched the Roman deployment. On his left
flank were the Spanish and Gallic cavalry,
resting on the river, next to them his heavy
infantry. The Gauls were thrown forward in
an arc, facing and extending beyond the
Roman front, with the Numidian cavalry on
his right flank. Being thinly spread, Hannibal's
40,000 infantry retained the tactical flexibility
to manoeuvre and slowly give ground before
the massed Roman legions; the arc would be
reversed to curve rearwards and as the
Romans pressed forward, they would be
enveloped. The risk was that the centre of the
arc would be torn apart, in which case the
battle would be lost, but Hannibal's cavalry
were superior both in number – some 10,000
– and quality, so could be relied upon to
defeat their Roman opponents and then
complete the encirclement. That is exactly
what happened. As the Romans pressed
forward, the Carthaginian infantry overlapped

their front and assaulted them on the flanks.
Compressed together and unable to protect
themselves, the casualties mounted and
the forward momentum began to falter.
Meanwhile the Roman cavalry had been
routed and the returning Numidians fell upon
the Roman rear. Completely surrounded and
still further compressed, the Romans were
slaughtered where they stood. According to
Polybius, only some 3,500 Romans managed
to escape, while 10,000 were taken prisoner
and 70,000 left dead on the battlefield.
Amongst those who escaped was the
perpetrator of the disaster, Varro; the
unfortunate Paulus was counted amongst
the dead.

After such an overwhelming victory the
question arises as to why Hannibal did not
then march on Rome. Instead he continued
to try to bring about the dissolution of the
Roman Confederation. Many explanations
are possible, but even with hindsight it
would be unwise to pass judgment on a
complex decision about which we only have
the most rudimentary knowledge. Before
following Hannibal any further, mention
should be made of the fact that though the
Romans had suffered grievously at home, the
two Scipio brothers, Gnaeus and Publius, had
landed in Spain and conducted a well-
executed land and sea campaign. However,
lacking the resources, they had been unable
achieve anything decisive.

The war expands 215–206 BC

When news of Hannibal's victory at Cannae reached Carthage, a wave of enthusiasm for the war swept through the city, ambitions rose and Hannibal's plans for broadening the canvas of the war were accepted. In essence Hannibal proposed a strategic encirclement of Italy, the execution of which would be the responsibility of the Carthaginian Senate, and an inner encirclement of Rome itself through the detachment of her allies, for which he would continue to be responsible. Whether this plan was conceived with a measured intellectual approach or, as seems more probable, opportunistically and pragmatically, is not known, but however arrived at, it was both grandiose and imaginative in its design. We already know Hannibal's operational concept for isolating Rome from her allies, but we need to look briefly at his wider strategic concept for the encirclement of the Italian peninsula.

With the succession of the 17-year-old Philip V to the Macedonian throne, the influence of Demetrius, who had taken refuge in the Macedonian court after losing his Illyrian possessions, weighed heavily in persuading Philip to side with the Carthaginians and evict the Romans from the Adriatic seaboard. Much the same situation arose to the south in Sicily, where Rome's ally Hiero of Syracuse had been succeeded by his 15-year-old grandson Hieronymus, who, under pressure from Hiero's two sons-in-law, agreed to enter into an alliance with Hannibal. To the west, in Sardinia, where a Carthaginian trading presence had long been amicably tolerated, a revolution was festering following the Romans' ruthless subjugation of the whole island after the First Punic War. With Carthaginian reinforcements assured for Spain, and the Romans' loss of an entire consular army against the Gauls to the north in 216 BC, given a fair share of good fortune and an adequate degree of competence in its execution, in the aftermath of Cannae the prospects for Carthaginian strategic encirclement looked favourable. The inner ring round Rome only required Hannibal to continue with his seemingly effortless succession of victories. What went wrong and why this double envelopment failed will now be examined theatre by theatre.

The campaign in Spain 215–206 BC

After receiving over 4,000 cavalry and infantry reinforcements and being relieved in southern Spain by a new army recently arrived from Carthage, Hasdrubal marched north to settle accounts with the Scipios. These two armies were of almost equal strength and when they met, in obvious imitation of his brother's tactics at Cannae, Hasdrubal thinned out the Spanish infantry, holding the centre, and concentrated the Libyans and cavalry on the wings. Hasdrubal was no Hannibal, however, and the Romans broke through his centre, destroyed his army and regained the line of the Ebro. After two years of inconclusive fighting the Scipios decided to divide their army between them; this dispersion of force resulted in them being handsomely defeated and counted amongst the dead. The opportunity for Hasdrubal to recover the whole of Spain came and went through internal dissension. Time was allowed for Roman reinforcements to arrive in 210 BC, including a new commander-in-chief, the 25-year-old military genius who was later to be known as Scipio Africanus, the son and nephew of the two Scipios who had been killed two years earlier. After rallying his disheartened troops, the following year Scipio struck at New Carthage rather than attacking the two Carthaginian armies lying near Gibraltar and Madrid, whose commanders were still not able to reconcile their differences and co-operate.

It took Scipio seven days to reach New Carthage, and he began his assault on the city almost immediately, from both land and sea. As the day matured and the casualties mounted with no prospect of success, Scipio sounded the retreat before making his next move, which would prove to be decisive. Learning from some fishermen that at ebb tide it was possible to

Nineteenth-century painting by Evariste Vital Luminais, showing a fight between Romans and Gauls. (Edimedia, Paris)

ford one of the lagoons and approach the city from the rear, Scipio sought surprise by deception. Renewing his assault on the section of the wall he had attacked the previous day, Scipio drew the defenders to what they regarded as the critical point while he led a 500-strong contingent across the lagoon and scaled the weakly defended northern wall. The city was soon secured, most of its citizens massacred and an immense amount of booty taken.

Following the fall of New Carthage, Scipio turned his attention to the field armies and in 208 BC Hasdrubal, after suffering a defeat on the headwaters of the Guadalquivir, inexplicably decided to join Hannibal in Italy. As we will see later, it was a fateful move, both for him personally and for those he commanded. Though substantial reinforcements had arrived from Carthage, in 206 BC the Carthaginians were finally defeated at Ilipa, some 10 miles north of modern Seville, to end the war in Spain. There

were two main causes for the Carthaginian defeat: first, their long enduring political dissension, reflecting the rivalry between the Barcids in Spain and those in power in Carthage; secondly, the superior generalship of Scipio. So much for Spain; we must now look and see what was happening elsewhere.

Sardinia 215 BC

In 215 BC, the year after Cannae, a small Carthaginian expedition sailed for Sardinia but ran into a violent storm and was blown off course to the Balearic Islands, where the ships had to be hauled ashore for repair. All this caused considerable delay, and by the time the Carthaginians reached Sardinia, the Romans had been alerted and had reinforced the island with a second legion, quickly suppressing a premature revolt. When the Carthaginians landed, little effective support was available and, lacking adequate strength by themselves, they were soon defeated. Their commander was taken prisoner and the

View of the river Rhône by Alexander Dunouy, . (Edimedia, Paris)

survivors were left with little alternative but to flee to their ships. Fate had not favoured the Carthaginians, but whether they would have prevailed otherwise is far from certain.

Sicily 215–210 BC

Hieronymus of Syracuse, who had inherited the throne and decided to side with the Carthaginians, was assassinated by members

of the pro-Roman party and for a time it looked as though Carthaginian intentions had been thwarted. However, the pro-Roman faction behaved with such wanton cruelty that they in turn were overthrown. This caused the Romans to reinforce Sicily, as in Sardinia, with a second legion. Syracuse now became the Romans' primary objective but with its formidable fortifications, which had been further strengthened by the ingenious war machines of Archimedes that could hurl boulders and grapple ships, it was no easy undertaking. Indeed, the first land and sea assault was a costly failure. Meanwhile the Carthaginians had sent formidable reinforcements. The situation looked critical for the Romans, until two further legions were sent, thus enabling them both to lay siege to Syracuse and to confront the newly arrived Carthaginians.

In 212 BC the Romans achieved a decisive victory. The Syracusans' enthusiastic indulgence during a religious festival had left them with unsteady legs and less than clear heads, and they were easily surprised. The Romans scaled the outer defences under cover of darkness to open one of the city's gates, and swarming in, the Romans soon established themselves in an unassailable position ringing the inner defences. Deserted by their fleet and so deprived of any relief, the garrison surrendered. Having secured the city it was given over to plunder by the Romans, who destroyed three centuries of civilisation and massacred the population, including Archimedes, one of the antique world's greatest mathematicians and physicists. With the fall of Syracuse the campaign seemed to be coming to an end, but the arrival of further Carthaginian reinforcements prolonged the struggle for another three years.

Unlike the First Punic War, the Carthaginians had made strenuous efforts and sent two reinforcing armies, together numbering nearly 40,000 men, besides

A third-century Roman mosaic showing the death of Archimedes. (Roger-Viollet)

constructing a powerful fleet and a large number of supply ships. Why then did they fail? It was quite simply a matter of poor generalship on both land and sea, but before rushing to crucify any surviving general, as was the Carthaginian wont, let us wait until the concluding analysis of this complex war is completed.

Illyria 215–205 BC

Unlike the other campaigns we have considered, there was no direct Carthaginian involvement in Illyria, so it was left to Philip of Macedon to try to drive the Romans from their foothold on the Adriatic coast. This task added a new dimension to Macedonian interests, which hitherto had been almost entirely concerned with the land-locked country's eastern and southern borders. With Macedonian manpower gravely depleted by the adventures of Alexander the Great, Philip was in no position to fight a war on more than one front. In order that he could turn against the Romans, a peace treaty had to be concluded with Aetolia, a powerful Greek state with which he was at war; but before Philip was ready to begin his campaign, he found himself under attack. The envoys he had despatched, informing Hannibal of his intentions, had been intercepted by the Romans, who now decided to reinforce their coastal garrison with an additional legion and take the initiative themselves.

Surprised by the sudden Roman move, Philip was caught off-balance and forced to withdraw, but in 213 BC he was able to go on to the offensive himself and secured several Roman allied coastal cities. Soon afterwards, however, he found himself marching and counter-marching, either to expel aggressors inspired by the Romans, including Aetolia, or to respond to appeals for help from his allies. This scrappy and exhausting campaign eventually came to an inconclusive end in 205 BC. Though Philip had won nearly all his tactical battles, he had apparently not appreciated the precariousness of his position at the

The Col d'Izoard, leading to the valley of Queyras, from which Hannibal was attacked. (Spectrum Colour Library)

An eighteenth-century engraving showing Archimedes' counter-weighted beams which snapped and capsized Roman warships in 212 BC. (Ann Ronan Picture Library)

The two armies confronted one another at Zama, some 100 miles south-west of Carthage. Though the Romans had a superiority in cavalry, overall numbers were probably about equal, some 40,000 apiece. Though it would be difficult to overestimate the importance of Zama, with the Carthaginians fighting for their lives and homeland and the Romans for the supremacy of their empire, as the two commanders appear to have matched one another tactically, the battle was little more than a grisly slogging match in which the Romans prevailed. The details then need not concern us, but what is of interest about Zama is how it demonstrated the interplay between the operational and strategic levels of war. By ravaging the Bagradas valley, Scipio had drawn Hannibal away from his own secure base into a hostile interior where he had to fight on ground and conditions not of his own choosing. This would have been a difficult operational situation to have created in Italy but, by taking the strategic decision to transfer the war to Africa, it was achieved almost effortlessly.

Hannibal had escaped from Zama and was able to exert a moderating influence on those who argued against accepting the Romans' inevitably harsher terms. The number of warships allowed was halved, the indemnity increased, and Punic military rights were drastically curtailed, leaving Carthage as little more than a client state of Rome. The war that had brought devastation to the whole of the Mediterranean during the previous 17 years had come to an end, leaving Rome as an imperial power of unmatched military might.

The following section deals with some of the major events which occurred during the next 50 years that led up to the Third Punic War, so all that needs to be said here is that when Scipio Africanus returned to Rome, he was indisputably the most powerful figure in the city. As political in-fighting tore reasonable compromise apart and the passage of time diminished Scipio's moderating influence, in 184 BC

he finally withdrew from public life in disgust.

The Third Punic War 149–146 BC

Carthage had been built on a naturally strong defensive position and then extensively fortified. There were only two restricted land approaches, either along the 3,000-yard wide isthmus to the north, protected by three lines of massive defence works towering one above the other, or along the narrow spit of sand to the south, which terminated at the foot of the city walls. The two isthmuses were separated by the unfordable Lake of Tunis and washed by the sea on their outer shores. The single 22-mile city wall enclosed the great harbour, the entrance of which lay just to the east of the southern sandbar, as well as the citadel constructed on the prominent Byrsa mound, not far from the harbour.

The Romans divided their forces between the two isthmuses, and when ready, attempted to carry these two directly approachable defence works by storm. Not surprisingly, they met with a bloody repulse in the north. Undeterred, they flung themselves forward for a second attempt that was equally unsuccessful. On the sandbar to the south they fared somewhat better. By using massive battering-rams propelled by several hundred soldiers and sailors, a breach was made in the city wall, but the assault troops failed to exploit the opportunity, so allowing the Carthaginians to throw up fresh barriers during the night and man the surrounding rooftops.

It was a brief respite. Though the Romans were met with a hail of missiles and were driven back, when they resumed the attack the following day an unseemly withdrawal was prevented from turning into a rout only by the timely intervention of Scipio Aemelianus, the adopted grandson of Scipio Africanus, who was serving as a tribune with the Fourth Legion. Roman impetuosity was then sharply curbed, and they settled down

A reconstruction of the circular inner harbour for warships at
Carthage (above), and the harbour as it is today. (AKG, Berlin)

The River Aufides (Ofante), with an ancient colonnade erected later, inscribed with a quotation from Livy:
'No other nation could have suffered such tremendous disasters and not been destroyed'.
(Sopraintendenza Archeologica delle Puglie, Taranto)

Stele, one of the remains of Carthage. (Roger-Viollet)

promoted to consul and given command in Africa. He at once set to work constructing a huge mole, which was to extend from the sandbar across the harbour mouth and bottle up the Carthaginian fleet, as well as sealing off any further supplies. At first the Carthaginians did not believe that the Romans could succeed, but as work progressed relentlessly, they took counter-measures and cut a new entrance from the inner harbour, giving access to the sea from the east. Fifty triremes then sailed out in a triumphal display of contempt; but it was an unwise gesture, as they lost the element of surprise and so the opportunity to destroy the Roman fleet, which was lying unmanned at anchor while the sailors toiled on the mole.

Nothing daunted, Scipio positioned his battering rams and other siege engines at the end of the now completed mole and made a partial breach, but during the night a Carthaginian raiding party swam out to the mole and set fire to the closely packed siege equipment. The Carthaginians then worked feverishly to repair the damage and raise additional towers along the wall. However, it was only a matter of time before the Romans had secured a foothold between the outer sea wall and that of the harbour, which enabled them to block the newly constructed harbour entrance. Cut off from both land and sea, Carthage's fate was sealed. While the preparations for the final assault were under way, Scipo took the opportunity to mount a mopping-up operation into the interior and extinguish the last flickering embers of Carthaginian resistance beyond their capital's crumbling defences.

The final assault was mounted from the harbour area where the Romans had established themselves the previous autumn. After some desperate fighting they managed to breach the city wall and then penetrate into the sprawling dockyard buildings, which the Carthaginians set alight once their strength began to fail. A new defensive line was adopted, centred primarily on the citadel

to the more prosaic business of blockading the city. The Carthaginians, however, did not rest on the defensive and made a determined sortie along the northern isthmus. Catching the Romans by surprise, they forced them to abandon their forward position in favour of one further back.

The following year, in 148 BC, although the Romans secured a number of small inland cities and others along the coast, the obvious lack of leadership, which had wasted the first two years of the war, led to demands for the appointment of a more vigorous commander. As a result, with the enthusiastic support of the Roman people and the army, Scipio Aemelianus was

Ruins of the Acropolis of Carthage. (Roger-Viollet)

Hannibal Barcid and Scipio Africanus

Since leadership plays such a vital part in all we have discussed, it seems appropriate to consider the qualities displayed by the two greatest leaders to emerge from the Punic Wars, Hannibal and Scipio; though it should be remembered that we have no contemporary assessments, only later, often unsubstantiated, opinions and, of course, accounts of their doings and sayings. This does not mean that we cannot attempt to piece together a picture of the two men, though it does mean the end result will be far from complete and in some aspects distorted, even perhaps to the extent of being factually incorrect.

Hannibal

In making any assessment of Hannibal's character and the force which motivated him to pursue war with such single-mindedness, it is essential to understand his background and upbringing. Born in 247 BC, Hannibal was only six years old when the First Punic War ended with his father's ignominious expulsion from Sicily. The event could hardly have affected him personally had it not been for his father's enduring determination to seek revenge. Slowly the enormity of the setback to Barcid pride and ambitions must have been conveyed to the boy, then it was indelibly stamped upon his conscience during a religious ceremony. In 237 BC, when Hannibal was 10 years old and his father was preparing to take his army to Spain, while propitiating the gods with a sacrifice, he took the opportunity to make his son swear an oath on the sacrificial animal that when he grew up, he would never forget that Rome was the deadly enemy. Once in Spain, the mould of Hannibal's character and motivating force behind his

life would have been forever cast. There could be no turning back, especially as Hannibal, like his father before him, was a warrior by nature.

Perhaps the highest tribute that can be paid to Hannibal's ability as a leader is to recognise the remarkable way in which he welded such a disparate force of unpatriotic mercenaries into a cohesive fighting force, inspired with self confidence and audacity, ready to face severe hardships and near unbelievable risks. Some of this loyalty can be ascribed to factors other than personal devotion, such as the way his father had been able to transform the various tribal superstitions into a mystical theology centred on the Barca family – they ruled by divine right – or, at the other end of the spectrum, the religious cynics, adventurers and materialists seeking plunder and rapine.

That Hannibal understood fully the capabilities and limitations of those he commanded is shown in the way he deployed them on the battlefield. At Cannae, for example, it was the tough and reliable Libyans whom he placed in the two key flank positions where the encircling movement was to be hinged; his dashing and opportunistic Numidian cavalry were deployed on his open right flank.

Hannibal always led by example, whether swimming a river first in Spain, to encourage his men to follow, or, as Livy tells us, sharing their hardships and living like an ordinary soldier when campaigning, always sleeping on the ground wrapped only in his military coat. However much Hannibal's own powerful personality was stamped upon his army, he knew how to decentralise authority, relying on the intimate group of generals who commanded its various components. Following the example of his father and the traditional Punic custom of nepotism,

Hannibal appointed his close relations to positions of responsibility, hence his brother Hasdrubal being left in charge in Spain. Natural leaders from outside his clan were also selected for command, such as the two great Numidian cavalry commanders, Carthalo and Maharbal, who protested at what they saw as Hannibal's excessive prudence in not marching on Rome after Cannae.

Having praised Hannibal for his soldierly qualities, Livy proceeds to list, though without preliminary evidence, his shortcomings, depicting him as 'excessively cruel, with a total disregard for the truth, honour and religion, for the sanctity of an oath and all that other men held sacred'. The charge of cruelty might be a matter of mistaken identity: one of Hannibal's commanders is alleged to have advocated that his soldiers should be trained to eat human flesh, thus easing the army's logistics problem. It is possible that this ferocious individual, named Hannibal Monomarchus, committed acts of cruelty that were mistakenly attributed to Hannibal himself.

Admittedly Hannibal must have shared many of the characteristics of a harsher age, but as a professional soldier he was undoubtedly a genius. His strategic vision threw the Romans on to the defensive and, for the first five years of the Second Punic War, permitted them to do little more than react to protect their homeland.

After the Third Punic War Hannibal was forced into exile, but wherever he sought refuge the Romans pursued him, accusing him of plotting against them – which he probably was – and demanded his extradition. Finally there was no way of escape. As Plutarch wrote, Hannibal was cornered 'like a bird that had grown too old to fly', a state of affairs Hannibal himself must have recognised since he made no attempt to escape, contenting himself with saying: 'Let us now put an end to the great anxiety of the Romans, who have thought it too lengthy and too heavy a task to wait for the death of a hated old man.' He took poison, and in 183 BC, at the age of 64, the scourge of the Romans departed this life.

Scipio Africanus

Though Scipio was only accorded the title of Africanus at the end of the Second Punic War upon entering Rome to receive the greatest triumph ever, he has been referred to as Africanus from the start, in order to save possible confusion with his father, Publius Cornelius Scipio, after whom he was named. Scipio was born in 235 BC. During his formative years he was greatly influenced by Greek philosophy and literature, but above all by Hellenistic rationalism which, combined with his instinctive pragmatism, induced a sceptical contempt for the superstitions of others. His tastes, however, were not all intellectual; he also appreciated the material comforts that the more advanced and sophisticated Greek civilisation had to offer. He later came under criticism from the *quaestor* (financial administrator) for his facility to imitate the Greeks and in so doing incur excessive expenses while

Third or second-century BC Carthaginian monument at Dugga, Tunisia. (Roger-Viollet)

Silver Carthaginian coin thought to show a portrait of
Hannibal. (Roger-Viollet)

preparing for the invasion of Africa. Scipio
promptly sent him packing with the words: 'I
do not like so exact a quaestor.'

Compared to his contemporaries, Scipio
must have been unusually liberal minded,
open to new ideas but still placing a high
value on both intellectual and moral values.
Perhaps he accepted the belief that by
performing just acts and acquiring good
habits, a man's character is formed and the
qualities of a leader established. His
moderation and sense of justice were
displayed by his attitude to Carthage after
her defeat, and his morality showed in his
behaviour to women after the capture of New

Carthage. On one occasion a young woman
of particular beauty was brought to Scipio by
some of his soldiers. Polybius relates how
Scipio 'was struck with admiration for her
beauty and replied that, if he had been a
private citizen, he would have received no
present which would have given him greater
pleasure, but as a general it was the last thing
in the world he could accept'. Polybius also
relates how after capturing New Carthage
Scipio refused to take anything for his own
private use, and when returning from Africa
allowed nothing to be mixed up with his
private property. Following his retirement,
however, he had a fracas with some officials
who had arrested his brother for financial
irregularities, whereupon Scipio released him,
destroyed the order for his arrest and said:

'I shall not give an account of four millions of sesterces when I put two hundred million into the treasury. For myself, I have only brought back the title of Africanus.'

The self-assurance Scipio displayed was in part derived from a sense of direct communion with the gods, especially with Jupiter, to whom he displayed a particular devotion and from whom, reflecting the Roman religious belief, he could expect reciprocal favours. A thoroughly realistic and pragmatic association far removed from the religious fanaticism that cleaves much of the world today.

Whereas Hannibal virtually disassociated himself from political machinations by maintaining his father's independent power base in Spain, Scipio found it necessary to enter into the political fray. With near impeccable credentials, as the son of a soldier killed on the battlefield, a participant in the first major clash with Hannibal after his crossing of the Alps and one of the few survivors of Cannae, Scipio presented himself at the Forum for election as an *aedile* (responsible for public works and activities), which was an essential preliminary to higher office. Here his youthful vigour and ardent convictions won the rapturous support of the people, long tired of endless defeat and yearning for an inspirational leader who would offer them hope for the future. Having been elected aedile, he later presented himself as a candidate for consular command of the army in Spain, and though there were some who resented this precocious youth, he was again elected.

Without detracting from his qualities, amongst which high intelligence and clarity of vision figured prominently, in many ways Scipio was fortunate in that opportunities presented themselves; unlike Hannibal, he did not have to create them. Had his father not been killed, Scipio would not have been given the chance to distinguish himself as a 25-year-old in Spain, and without that achievement he would not have been given command of an army and entrusted to carry the war to Africa. When coming face to face with Hannibal he was still a young man with the full vigour of his youth, whereas Hannibal had already been campaigning for 17 consecutive years in Italy. It is not unreasonable to suppose the years had taken their toll on Hannibal, both physically and mentally, and we should perhaps not discount the possibility of Hannibal feeling a bit below par at Zama.

As we have seen, however, Scipio's good fortune did not endure after his retirement. For the first few years his reputation put him above the political in-fighting with which he was surrounded, but as time passed his critics became more vocal until he went into voluntary exile at Liternium, a disillusioned and embittered man, forgotten by the country which he had set on the path to universal conquest of the known world. He died in 183 BC at the age of 52, and though there are memorials to him in both Rome and Liternium, he has no known grave.

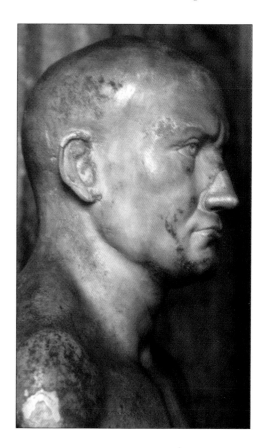

A bronze statue of Scipio Africanus. (Edimedia, Paris)

The political, social and economic impact

In this chapter we will look at the effects of the war on the civilian population though, as has already been mentioned, since there are no Carthaginian records and because the ancient historians only lightly touched upon such matters, our examination can be neither even-handed nor complete. Though much will then be left to the reader to draw his own conclusions, we can at least try to get a feel for the situation as it affected the ordinary people.

The Carthaginians

During the First Punic War Hanno the Great, the leader of the aristocratic party in Carthage, who was implacably opposed to the overseas expansionist policies of Hamilcar Barca and the Barcid party, was authorised to exploit the Carthaginian agrarian empire in North Africa. This extension of the Libyan conquests, coupled with the task of subduing unrest amongst the Numidians while simultaneously maintaining a substantial fleet and sustaining the campaign in Sicily, was more than even the well-stocked Carthaginian treasury could afford. An attempt was made to negotiate a loan from Ptolemy II of Egypt, but he sagaciously declined on the grounds that he was a friend of both the Carthaginians and the Romans. One of these undertakings then had to be renounced, and since Hanno would not have contemplated restricting his African enterprises and found it virtually impossible to extricate the army in Sicily, he took the easiest option and withdrew the fleet. Divided political interests then assured the Romans of naval superiority in Sicilian waters and, ultimately, of victory. We do not know if the financial burden of campaigning weighed down on the Carthaginian people as a whole,

or whether it was just the aristocratic landowners who were suffering, but wherever it fell, the mere fact that an attempt was made to raise an overseas loan indicates that the crisis was real enough.

As we have seen the Mercenary Revolt which followed the First Punic War arose because the Carthaginians were unwilling to pay the mercenaries their due. The enthusiasm with which the African cities threw in their lot with the mercenaries was largely due to the harshness of the treatment they had received during the closing years of the war. Persuaded that the exigencies of the situation justified such measures, the Carthaginians had commandeered one half of the annual produce of the lands throughout their subject territories and doubled the annual tribute imposed upon the cities. No compunction was shown in extorting these dues, regardless of the devastating consequences for those living by a subsistence economy. Small wonder that the young men flocked to join the revolt, while the women and others who remained behind met together and solemnly swore not to conceal any of their possessions but to offer them all to the common cause. As a result, the two leaders of the revolt, Spendius and Matho, were not only able to complete the payment of arrears due their men, but from that time on were able to defray the cost of the uprising. This suggests that the cause of such deep resentment was not so much the actual raising of the money by the Carthaginians as the harshness and indiscriminate manner in which it was done.

According to Polybius, the Carthaginians were by then nearly exhausted by the demands of the recent prolonged war and found themselves without any revenue to support an army. The situation cannot have been quite this forlorn since shortly afterwards the Carthaginians were able to take the field in considerable strength, obtain new mercenaries, refit their surviving warships, arm all their able-bodied citizens, raise a new force of cavalry and muster the 100 elephants remaining to them. Again, in the absence of any Carthaginian records, to attempt to comment on the true situation and the extent of the suffering endured by the Carthaginian people themselves would be sheer speculation.

After Hamilcar Barca had established himself in Spain, the wealth there not only enabled him to meet his own requirements but also to replenish the Carthaginian coffers and recompense the authorities of Gades (Cadiz) for their loyalty when he had first crossed from Africa. We do not know the relative proportion of these three allocations, but the amount supplied to Carthage must have been considerable: not only did it enable the war debt to be paid off to Rome, but it provided discreet payments to political supporters.

The political effect of the First Punic War had been to weaken the position of the great landowners who favoured good relations with Rome. The merchants now saw the riches of Sicily flowing into the Roman treasury instead of into their own pockets, and the secure sea routes throughout the Mediterranean threatened, if not actually broken; the commercial domination they had enjoyed was dissolving before their eyes. But it was not just the merchants who were discontented. The war with Rome had virtually destroyed the navy and put a large number of Carthaginian citizens connected with maritime activities out of work. The disquiet of these classes provided a strong undercurrent of support for those like Hamilcar Barca who advocated expansion overseas. After the end of the Second Punic War, the pendulum swung back, bringing the big landowners into power. The commercial classes, and even the Barcid faction, which had supported first Hamilcar Barca and then Hannibal, now accepted the realities of the situation and sought an enduring accommodation with Rome. However harsh the peace terms and

however reduced the opportunities for trade, the prospect of prosperous commercial activity still remained.

The Romans

It was the succession of maritime disasters, resulting in the loss of at least 500 fully manned warships and 1,000 transports which saw the First Punic War reach a low ebb for the Romans. Not only did the state face bankruptcy and exhaustion, but a population census showed a fall of some 17 per cent, excluding the allies. To call for new taxes and further levies of manpower risked social unrest, and in 247 BC political change became inevitable. The Fabii, with their policy of moderation towards Carthage in favour of their northern landed interests, were exerting increasing influence over public opinion, while the Claudii, who stood to gain more from southern expansion, were becoming discredited and faced accusations of impiety – perhaps given substance by Claudius Pulcher, the member of the Claudian clan who cast the sacred chickens overboard after they failed to provide a favourable omen.

Perhaps the most significant political development followed the acquisition of Sicily at the end of the First Punic War. Hitherto the Romans had never exacted payments in cash or kind from subjected territories, but instead demanded military service from those they termed as allies and with whom they shared the spoils of war. Now, however, they found it more convenient to adapt the entire concept of government to the existing administrative system in Sicily: they would impose a tribute and rely on self-administration through bureaucratically appointed councils, while providing the military garrisons themselves. These measures elevated Rome from mere leader of an Italian Confederation to an imperial power.

There was also an important internal political consequence of the First Punic War. As had occurred in the past, new plebeian families who had distinguished themselves were elevated to the Senate. Though this did not lead to the creation of an influential military faction, it did mean that consulships were distributed with greater political and social evenness, though it is difficult to identify any improvement in the quality of leadership. Varro, who was responsible for the disaster of Cannae, had been elected by the plebeian party as their representative.

The losses at Cannae had caused unprecedented terror and confusion in Rome. Only the previous year a consul and his army had been lost at Trasimene and now two more had suffered the same fate, leaving Rome without an army in the field, no commander of distinction and most of Italy overrun. In an attempt to calm the population, the Senate forbade women to leave their houses; they were to remain at home where they would be informed of their personal losses. Silence was imposed everywhere, family mourning was strictly curtailed and the city gates were closed to keep the people in as well as Hannibal out. As if the military disasters had not been enough, an act of gross impiety added to the general alarm. Two of the Vestal Virgins, charged with keeping the sacred flame in the temple of Vesta alight, were convicted for illicit sexual activity. One of them committed suicide and the other was buried alive, while the debaucher, the Lesser Pontiff, was beaten to death by no less a personage than the *Pontifex Maximus* himself. Similar panic and turmoil occurred a few years later when Hannibal was trying to relieve pressure on Capua by marching on Rome. The fearful cry of *Hannibal ad portas* rang through the city and exaggerated reports abounded. Weeping and wailing women ran aimlessly around the shrines, sweeping the altars with their loosened hair and appealing to the gods to save them and their children.

As the war dragged on, people sought solace in the superstitions of eastern cults. Instead of worshipping in the privacy of their homes, crowds of women thronged the forum and other public places where they offered sacrifices and prayers in accordance with unaccustomed rites. This gullibility gave

rise to a new breed of soothsayers and prophets who were quick to exploit the opportunity for personal gain. Of more immediate concern to the Senate, however, was the demand for new recruits. Commissioners were appointed, charged with searching for those fit to bear arms, even if this meant enrolling boys below the age of 17, while slaves were recruited and criminals released from prison to fill the depleted ranks of the legions.

Towards the end of the Second Punic War, shortly before Hannibal was recalled to Carthage, the Senate strove to achieve a return to normality and, in particular, to get the people back on to the land. This proved to be no easy task, since most of the free

farmers had been killed in the war, slaves were scarce, cattle had been carried off and farm buildings destroyed. It was against this backdrop that Scipio had to persuade an anxious Senate to permit him to carry the war to Africa. Concern was expressed about the social consequences for the Roman people should he enter into a decisive battle against his formidable opponent, especially on his home ground. There was also the matter of public opinion to be considered: how would the Roman people and their allies react to the inevitable demands for additional manpower and resources to open up a new theatre of war? Twelve of the Latin colonies had already refused to make any further contributions, and the people had shown how near to exhaustion they had become, but after referring the issue to the people, the Senate, somewhat evasively, granted Scipio his request so long as he judged it to be in the interests of the state.

From all this it is apparent that the Romans remained a cohesive society in spite of the appalling losses they suffered in human lives and material resources. We may not know of any individual cases, but it is not hard to imagine what it must have been like for the many thousands of families deprived of their bread-winner and with no state aid to fall back on.

Remains of the house of the Vestal Virgins in Rome. The statues are those of high priestesses. (AKG, Berlin)

Carthaginian trade; a Roman senator

The only Carthaginian politician of prominence was Hanno the Great, but as so little is known about him, his personality lies beyond our reach; we will look instead at Carthaginian trade and colonisation, which were closely linked, the latter generally following the former, to create the bedrock of their civilisation.

It should be appreciated that the Mediterranean climate during the third century BC was very different from that of today, affecting to some extent both what was traded and so the siting of settlements. North Africa, for example, was thickly wooded and supported a multitude of game such as elephants, lions, panthers and bears, while Sicily produced an abundance of wheat, vines and honey. Similarly, the Bible refers to Palestine as 'a land flowing in milk and honey', which is confirmed by bore holes sunk in the former Lake Hula by the Israelis, showing evidence of seeds and cultivation which died out in subsequent centuries.

Reflecting a more highly developed civilisation than was general throughout the Mediterranean, the Phoenicians exported manufactured articles such as household furnishings of ivory-inlaid cedar, bronze and silver bowls, jewellery, glass vessels, purple cloth and small practical utensils like tweezers and razors. Imports supplied the raw materials – precious stones, ivory, gold, silver, copper and tin, the last two providing the alloy from which many of the utensils were made.

Trade was not confined to importing raw materials and exporting finished wares and products. Amongst many other things, Phoenician ships carried gold and silver to Greece and slaves to Near Eastern markets, while amphorae from Carthage were used for transporting wine and olive oil throughout the Mediterranean.

Herodotus tells us how the Carthaginians conducted their trade.

They unloaded their goods, arranged them tidily along the beach and after returning to their boats raised smoke. Seeing the smoke, the natives then came down to the beach, placed a certain amount of gold on the ground in exchange for the goods and then withdrew. The Carthaginians then came ashore and if they thought the gold represented a fair price, they collected it and took it and went away; if on the other hand they thought it too little, they would go back on board and wait. The natives would then come and add to the gold until they were satisfied. There was perfect harmony on both sides, the Carthaginians never touched the gold until it equalled in value what they had offered for sale, and the natives never touched the goods until the gold had been taken away.

Clearly this primitive sort of commerce could not endure, so first trading settlements were established and then colonies similar to Carthage itself.

Diodorus Siculus gives an insight into how this development occurred in Spain.

The country has the most numerous and excellent silver mines ... The natives do not know how to use the metal, but the Phoenicians, experts in commerce, would buy the silver in exchange for some other small goods. Consequently, taking the silver to Greece, Asia and other people, the Phoenicians made great earnings. Thus practising the trade for a long time, they became rich and founded many colonies, some in Sicily and on the neighbouring islands, others in Libya, Sardinia and Iberia.

Following the pattern of their trade, Carthaginian colonies were mainly established along the coast on promontories or small coastal islands facing lagoons of no great depth as their ships only required a shallow draught. The Greek colonies, on the other hand, which were being established at much the same time, were mostly sited inland, reflecting the Greeks' agricultural and more localised commercial interests.

To end this short survey we will take a look at Carthage itself, leaving aside the fortifications which have already been described. As a maritime nation the port was of supreme significance and consisted of two interconnecting harbours. The inner circular harbour was for warships and the outer rectangular one for merchant vessels. It will be remembered that when access through the mercantile harbour was blocked by Scipio, a new outlet was cut from the inner harbour from which the warships sailed in a display of contempt for the Roman endeavour. Outside the city itself, Diodorus Siculus describes the surrounding countryside as abounding with fruit trees and vines, irrigated by sluices and canals, pastured with sheep, herds of cattle and breeding mares and populated by villages displaying the wealth of their owners. No doubt, as in any society, there was also an unseemly side, but the overall picture is one of great prosperity bordering on luxury.

Marcus Cato, the scourge of Carthage. (Roger-Viollet)

Marcus Cato

At the same time as the Scipios were being fêted with triumphs, Marcus Cato arose who, amongst many other things, was to be the patrician family's greatest critic. It will be remembered how Scipio Africanus summarily dismissed Cato as his *quaestor* for criticising Scipio's extravagance while preparing for the African expedition. This was far from being an isolated incident. As a red-headed young man with penetrating blue eyes but of near barbaric appearance, Cato could alarm both friend and foe alike. He was so precocious that in his childhood he was called Cato (*Catus*, 'wise'), though his family, presumably because of his appearance, called him *Porcius* (swineherd). He seemingly did not have an easy start to life: able, but born into an undistinguished family when society was dominated by the aristocracy, he was driven by a near demonic energy to succeed and had an unquenchable desire for recognition, ambitions which called for rigorous single-mindedness and relentless self-discipline. Already gifted with a robust constitution, Cato further hardened himself physically by manual labour; sharing the hardships of those with whom he worked on the land, living frugally, drinking the same wine as his slaves and purchasing only the simplest of food in the market. He indulged in none of the excesses associated with youthful ardour, but instead prepared himself for higher purposes in life, becoming increasingly attracted to the ideals of simplicity and self-discipline, while practising and perfecting his oratory by appearing as an advocate for all who needed him without demanding a fee.

Like all those seeking political careers, Cato first served in the army and at the age of 17 saw active service in Spain, being wounded and distinguishing himself for his gallantry. However, according to Plutarch: 'He never stinted his own praise, and could never resist following up a great achievement without a boastful description of it.' From this it seems reasonable to conclude that self-advertisement prompted him to sell his horse, rather than incur public expenditure in transporting it back to Italy. If his motive really had been public economy, he could have paid the cost himself, but this would have attracted little attention, except perhaps cynical disbelief.

Cato's treatment of his slaves also suggests a callous ruthlessness – he sold them when they became too old to work. As Plutarch said:

I regard exploiting them to the limits of their strength, and then, when they were old, driving them off and selling them, as a mark of a thoroughly ungenerous nature ...
A kindly man will take good care of his horses even when they are worn out in his services, and will look after his dogs not only when they are puppies, but when they need special attention in their old age.

Though Cato is alleged to have been a good father and a kind husband, his deep suspicion of Greek physicians who practised in Rome, and perhaps his own frugality, led him to treat his family and slaves himself when they fell sick. The results were hardly reassuring. Both his wife and son died of disease, as probably did other unfortunate members of his household. His own physique had a more enduring quality as even in advanced age he continued to indulge his sexual appetite, first comforting himself with a slave girl, then marrying the young daughter of one of his secretaries, much to the surprise of the latter, who regarded Cato as being well past the age of marriage.

Cato's most enduring, if discreditable, reputation is for contributing to the destruction of Carthage, not in the military sense but as a result of his advocacy. Returning from a diplomatic mission to North Africa, Cato warned the Senate that the crushing defeats the Carthaginians had suffered had done little to impair their strength or diminish their recklessness and over-confidence. They remained a potent threat to Rome. He ended his speech by dropping some gloriously over-sized

figs on to the floor of the Senate-house, declaring that where they came from was only three days' sail from Rome. Henceforth he continually rubbed in the point whenever

Relief of a Carthaginian merchant ship. (Roger-Viollet)

his opinion was called for on any subject, by concluding with the words: 'And furthermore it is my opinion that Carthage must be destroyed.' He never lived to see his wish fulfilled, dying shortly after the Third Punic War began. He was an austere, single-minded and ruthless man, but one who possessed both physical and moral courage.

Lxpansionism and the disposition for war

Since the history of the Punic Wars is written almost entirely from a military point of view, inevitably the conclusions will also be military. The consequences, however, which will be considered at the end of this chapter are not so restricted. But let us first look at the causes for war, then briefly consider its conduct by both antagonists, before drawing a broad conclusion as to why the Carthaginians were vanquished.

The causes of war are seldom explicit or simple, nor do they lend themselves to broad generalisations, such as commercial rivalry, social unrest or religious fanaticism. Usually there are also a number of interacting, if subsidiary, factors. These can include national or individual ambitions, prejudices and fears, all heightened by a generous measure of misunderstanding and miscalculation. To isolate one of these factors risks over-simplification, while to follow several can result in confusion.

Then there are the theorists: some consider war to be a cyclical process, the revulsion of a generation which has participated in a prolonged conflict being replaced by the romantic ardour of the next. Others put forward the theory of delinquency: nations are human beings writ large who inevitably squabble and then fight. A third group believes that wars arise from ignorance, which, through increased commercial, personal, cultural and other contacts, can be abolished. Although such explanations all contain elements of truth, in the light of experience none has given grounds for thinking that it is capable of standing alone.

If so much contemporary analysis and theorising has been devoted to determining the causes of war, it may well be asked what purpose will be served by considering what happened over 2,000 years ago. The available

evidence is fragmentary, the opinions expressed often hearsay, even at the time, and the relevance of such distant events is questionable. Even so, there are two clearly identifiable factors which made the First Punic War more probable and remain just as relevant today. First, the Romans saw an opportunity to gain a foothold in Sicily by aiding the Mamertines; and secondly, because they saw that the Carthaginians were unprepared militarily, they succumbed to the temptation.

The seemingly obvious cause of the Second Punic War was Hannibal's determination to avenge the loss of Sicily and his father's humiliation. This was certainly the immediate cause of the war but the overall setting was far more complex. There was an undeniable momentum behind Roman expansion: periods of peace were temporary interludes to be broken when a favourable opportunity for advancement presented itself. So it was with Sardinia, which the Romans seized in 238 BC and then unconvincingly claimed that it was one of the islands referred to as 'lying between Sicily and Italy' ceded to them following the First Punic War. In Italy itself, the Romans annexed Ager Gallicus on the Adriatic coast from the Gauls and incorporated the Etruscans into their confederation. Given Rome's clear cultural disposition for war, another conflict with Carthage was inevitable, only the timing was uncertain until decided by Hannibal.

The cause of the Third Punic War can be attributed to the loss of Scipio Africanus' moderating influence when he fell victim to political in-fighting, and his replacement by Cato with his advocacy of vigorous confrontation with Carthage. We can see the timelessness of these events by looking back to the Cold War, when the Soviets incorporated most of Eastern Europe into their brand of confederation, attempted to secure Berlin by blockade and drew down the Iron Curtain. Fortunately the West was more able to defend itself against confrontation than was Carthage.

Looking at the events of the three Punic Wars, we can see how important it is to adjust force structures to changing political and military requirements, and then to conduct war with a purposeful strategic aim. As we have seen, the Romans began a war which clearly had a major maritime dimension without possessing a navy, while the Carthaginians had an army which, without a long period of mobilisation, was incapable of defending its widely dispersed possessions. Then there was the direction of the war itself. The Romans initially had the limited, short-term objective of securing a foothold in Sicily; but by failing to define their long-term aim, they drifted into a prolonged conflict.

In the Second Punic War the Romans were initially thrown on to the defensive by Hannibal's superior generalship, until he lacked the strength to maintain the offensive and defend the cities he had gained. Ultimately the Romans prevailed on the battlefield because, however incompetent and divided the leadership was at times, military service formed a part of every aspiring citizen's upbringing. In sharp contrast, the Carthaginian politicians were mainly merchants, irreconcilably divided between those wishing to preserve their overseas interests by opposing Rome and those wanting to compromise in order to expand their African possessions. This was a political division which precluded any clear strategic national aim. In the end it was this, together with the inattention paid in peace-time to the provision and training of competent commanders, that led to Carthage's downfall rather than, as has sometimes been suggested, the Romans' greatly superior human and material resources.

Finally, let it be repeated: human nature does not change, only the circumstances with which it is surrounded. We should then never be led astray by wishful thinking, especially about totalitarian regimes, as was Chamberlain by Hitler at Munich, and Roosevelt by Stalin at Yalta; both were deceived and ultimately betrayed at terrible cost.

Since Carthage was obliterated and its population dispersed, it is only the Romans with whom we are concerned, so we cannot do better than begin by relating the prediction made by Scipio Africanus' grandson, Scipio Nasica. Shortly before the Third Punic War he warned the Senate that though Rome's position as a dominant power should be preserved, Carthage should not be destroyed as a rival. Were this to occur, there would be no check to Rome's arrogant disregard for the legitimate interests and concerns of smaller states. Moreover, in the absence of any external threat, the Roman Confederation would be in danger of disintegrating as fractious political and social groups pursued their own self-interested ends. Events proved Scipio's prediction to be remarkably perspicacious.

With ruthless determination the Romans extended their boundaries to the Euphrates, Danube, Rhine and Atlantic Ocean. A single city had expanded into an immense empire, but its arrogance brought its nemesis. The legions were no longer a citizen militia controlled by the Senate and enrolled to meet a passing need, but a long-service force of independent contingents whose loyalties had been transferred from a distant state to its immediate military commanders, many of whom had political ambitions. So it was in 49 BC when, at the head of five cohorts, Caesar crossed the Rubicon, the river marking the boundary between Cisalpine Gaul and Roman Italy, to unleash a civil war which was to extend from the Italian peninsula to Greece, Syria and Cappadocia, down through Africa, Sicily and Sardinia to Spain. Internecine struggles first weakened then extinguished the military vigour of the Roman world until Rome itself was sacked in AD 410 by Alaric the Visigoth.

The relentless expansion of the Roman Empire transformed the social and economic fabric of the Italian Confederation as the spoils of war poured into Italy. While the young men were drafted into the legions deployed along the empire's distant frontiers, they were replaced by tens of thousands of slaves who worked on the land or in domestic service. This could include concubinage, as was provided for Cato, or more debauching vices such as paedophilia, a practice acquired from the Greeks. But as time passed many slaves were enfranchised and became Roman citizens, though judging by Scipio Aemelianus' rebuke of those once thronging the Forum – 'Silence, spurious sons of Italy!' – of intemperate if not insolent behaviour. Thus a new breed of people arose who, holding different beliefs, customs and expectations, frequently rejected the social discipline and solid virtues practised by their Roman predecessors.

There had been an equally traumatic shift in economic conditions. Much of the new-found wealth found its way into the pockets of the powerful, including members of the Senate, who bought up land which they then worked with slave labour, displacing those peasant farmers who remained. The resulting impoverishment of the peasant class was further aggravated by long-serving soldiers being obliged to surrender land which they were unable to manage, leaving them homeless and destitute once they had completed their military service. A resentful class of Rome's once-loyal citizens then swelled the ranks of those seeking social justice. In 133 BC Tiberius Gracchus, a tribune and bold reformer, was assassinated for attempting to reverse this trend, as was his younger brother Gaius, when he tried to revive the reform. In this way the old inculcated Roman virtues of uprightness and duty to the state slipped into a decline marked by selfishness and insatiable greed.

In spite of the wealth that had flowed into Italy following the Romans' overseas conquests, its misappropriation and economic mismanagement necessitated higher taxes, a burden that was shifted by the rich and powerful on to the poorer classes, who, as Gibbon expressed it, 'bore the weight without sharing the benefits of society'. The rot at home invited the intervention of ambitious overseas commanders who, as we have seen, were not slow to pursue their own interests.

So Scipio Nasica's second prediction was fulfilled: internal disintegration would follow from the defeat of Carthage; a disintegration which ultimately led to the collapse of the Roman Empire. On the positive side, however, we should recall that Rome's defeat of Carthage paved the way for Western civilisation and the establishment of the Christian religion. For a brief period Rome unified most of modern-day Europe, to such an extent that, though the centre of gravity has shifted northwards, it is comparable with what is occurring some 2,000 years later. Gibbon, however, had harsh words to say about the impact of Christianity:

The clergy successfully preached the doctrines of patience and pusillanimity; the active virtues of society were discouraged; and the last remains of the military spirit were buried in the cloister; a large portion of private and public wealth was consecrated to the specious demands of charity and devotion.

However, to balance this critical assessment, he went on to say:

The pure and genuine influence of Christianity may be traced to its beneficial, though imperfect, effects on the Barbarian proselytes of the North. If the decline of the Roman Empire was hastened by the conversion of Constantine, his virtuous religion broke the violence of the fall, and mollified the ferocious temper of the conquerors. This awful revolution may be usefully applied to the instruction of the present age.

A knowledge of history plays an important part in understanding how we got where we are and in helping us to decide what we should do in the future; which brings us back to Polybius' contention, quoted at the beginning of this book: 'There are two sources from which any benefit can be derived; our own misfortunes and those which have happened to other men.'

Glossary of names

Agathocles Tyrant of Syracuse who eluded the Carthaginian siege of the city and carried the war into their North African homeland. He died in 289 BC.

Archimedes The most famous mathematician and physicist in antiquity. Native of Syracuse, whose war machines devastated the Roman fleet during the siege in which he was killed when the city fell in 212 BC.

Cato Roman senator who fought in Spain. His implacable hatred of Carthage was a major cause of the Third Punic War and the city's destruction.

Fabius, Maximus Quintus Roman consul nicknamed *Cunctator* (Delayer) because he shadowed Hannibal in the Second Punic War, hoping to wear him down without giving battle.

Flaminius, Gaius Roman consul killed with most of his men at the battle of Lake Trasimene in 217 BC, when trapped by Hannibal.

Hamilcar Barca Father of Hannibal. Commanded the Carthaginian forces in Sicily during the First Punic War. Suppressed the Mercenary Revolt in Africa (240–237 BC). Created an independent power base in Spain, where he was drowned when trying to escape across a river.

Hannibal Son of Hamilcar Barca. Secured the family base in Spain after the death of his father. Led his army from Spain over the Alps into Italy to begin the Second Punic War. After being called back to defend Carthage, he was defeated by Scipio Africanus at Zama in 202 BC.

Hanno (The Great) Leader of the aristocratic party in Carthage from 240–200 BC. Favoured development of the African provinces, so was the chief opponent of Hannibal and the Barcid party seeking overseas expansion.

Hanno Carthaginian general sent to Sicily at the outbreak of the First Punic War. Defeated at the naval battle of Ecnomus in 256 BC.

Hasdrubal Barca Left in command in Spain when his brother Hannibal crossed the Alps to campaign in Italy at the beginning of the Second Punic War. Later tried to join Hannibal but was killed on the Metaurus in 207 BC.

Hiero King of Syracuse who sided with the Carthaginians over the Mamertine problem in 264 BC but after being defeated by the Romans, changed sides and gave his allegiance to the latter. Remained a faithful Roman ally until his death in about 214 BC.

Maharbal Numidian cavalry general who crossed the Alps with Hannibal in 218 BC. Fought at the battles of Trasimene in 217 BC and Cannae in 216 BC.

Marcellus, Marcus Claudius Four times consul and Rome's most vigorous field commander in Sicily and Italy during the Second Punic War. Took Syracuse but was killed in battle in 208 BC.

Paulus, Lucius Armilius Roman consul sharing dual command with Varro at the battle of Cannae, where he fell in 216 BC.

Philip V King of Macedonia who entered into an alliance with Hannibal during the Second Punic War in 225 BC. Driven out of Illyria by the Romans and finally defeated in the Second Macedonian War in 192 BC.

Regulus, Marcus Atilius Roman consul who defeated the Carthaginians in the naval battle of Ecnomus in 256 BC. Invaded North Africa, where he was defeated by Xanthipus in the following year.

Scipio, Gnaeus Cornelius Uncle of Scipio Africanus. Killed with his brother Publius Cornelius Scipio in Spain in 211 BC.

Scipio, Publius Cornelius Roman consul and father of Scipio Africanus. Carried the campaign to Spain in the Second Punic War, where he was defeated and killed with his brother Gnaeus Cornelius Scipio in 211 BC.

Scipio Africanus After the deaths of his father and uncle in battle, he was given command of the Roman army in Spain in 209 BC and captured New Carthage. Landed in Africa in 204 BC and defeated Hannibal at Zama two years later.

Scipio, Nasica Grandson of Scipio Africanus who, after the Second Punic War, tried to persuade the Senate that it was in Rome's own interest not to destroy Carthage.

Spendius Roman deserter who, with the Libyan Matho, led the Mercenary Revolt in 240 BC.

Syphax King of Numidia who sided with the Carthaginians and was defeated in the Great Plains by Scipio Africanus and Masinissa in 209 BC.

Varro, Marcus Terentius Roman consul sharing command with Lucius Armilius Paulus but under whose direction the battle of Cannae was fought and lost in 216 BC.

Xanthipus Spartan mercenary who trained and led the Carthaginian army which defeated the Romans under Marcus Atilius Regulus in North Africa during the First Punic War in 255 BC.

Further reading

Primary sources

Bagnall, N.T., *The Punic Wars*, London (1990)

Bartoloni, P., 'Ships and Navigation', in *The Phoenicians*, Milan (1988)

Bartoloni, P., 'Commerce and Industry' in *The Phoenicians*, Milan (1988)

Blaney, G., *The Causes of War*, London (1978)

Bondi, S.F., 'City Planning', in *The Phoenicians*, Milan (1988)

Bondi, S.F., *Cambridge Ancient History* (Vols VII and VIII), Cambridge (1991)

Caven, B., *The Punic Wars*, London (1980)

Michelet, J., *The Roman Republic*, London (1847)

Moscati, S.,'Colonization of the Mediterranean', in *The Phoenicians*, Milan (1988)

Plutarch, *Makers of Rome*, London (1965)

Polybius, *The Histories*, London 1899)

Smith, R.B., *Carthage and the Carthaginians*, London (1890).

Thiel, J.H., *A History of Roman Sea Power*, Amsterdam (1954)

Other references

Adcock, F.E., *The Roman Art of War*, Cambridge, Mass (1940)

Arnold, T., *The Second Punic War*, London (1886)

Cicero, *The Offices*, London (1894)

De Beer, G., *Hannibal*, London (1969)

Diodorus, S., *Corpus Historicum*, London (1700)

Gibbon, E., *The Decline and Fall of the Roman Empire*, London (1775)

Grimal, P., *The Civilization of Rome*, London & New York (1963)

Harris, W., *War and Imperialism in Ancient Rome*, London (1979)

Herodotus, *The Histories*, London (1962)

Liddel, Hart B., *A Greater than Napoleon*, Edinburgh and London (1926)

Livy, *The Early History of Rome*, London (1965)

Livy, *Rome and Italy*, London (1965)

Livy, *The War with Hannibal*, London (1965)

Mahan, A.T., *The Influence of Sea Power on History*, London (1980)

Momsen, T., *The History of Rome*, New York (1987)

Picard, G.C., *The Life and Death of Carthage*, London (1968)

Ribichini, S., 'Beliefs and Religious Life', in *The Phoenicians*, Milan (1988)

Rollin, B.M., *The Ancient Histories*, Edinburgh, (1825)

Scullard, H., *The History of the Roman World*, London (1953)

Scullard, H., *Scipio Africanus*, New York (1970)

Schuckburgh, E., *The Histories of Polybius*, London (1899)

Wallbank, F., *Polybius: an Historical Commentary*, Oxford (1957)

Index

Other titles in the Essential Histories series

The Crusades
ISBN 1 84176 179 6

The Crimean War
ISBN 1 84176 186 9

The Seven Years'
War
ISBN 1 84176 191 5

The Napoleonic
Wars (1) The rise of
the Emperor 1805–1807
ISBN 1 84176 205 9

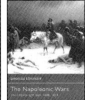

The Napoleonic
Wars (2) The empires
fight back 1808–1812
ISBN 1 84176 298 9

The French
Revolutionary Wars
ISBN 1 84176 283 0

Campaigns of the
Norman Conquest
ISBN 1 84176 228 8

The American Civil
War (1) The war in the
East 1861–May 1863
ISBN 1 84176 239 3

The American Civil
War (2) The war in the
West 1861–July 1863
ISBN 1 84176 240 7

The American Civil
War (3) The war in the
East 1863–1865
ISBN 1 84176 241 5

The American Civil
War (4) The war in the
West 1863–1865
ISBN 1 84176 242 3

The Korean War
ISBN 1 84176 282 2

The First World War
(1) The Eastern Front
1914–1918
ISBN 1 84176 342 X
January 2002

The First World War
(2) The Western Front
1914–1916
ISBN 1 84176 347 0
January 2002

The Punic Wars
264–146 BC
ISBN 1 84176 355 1
February 2002

The Falklands
War 1982
ISBN 1 84176 422 1
February 2002

The Napoleonic Wars
(3) The Peninsular War
1807–1814
ISBN 1 84176 370 5
March 2002

The Second World
War (1) The Pacific
ISBN 1 84176 229 6
March 2002

The Iran-Iraq War
1980–1988
ISBN 1 84176 371 3
April 2002

The French Religious
Wars 1562–1598
ISBN 1 84176 395 0
June 2002

The First World War
(3) The Western Front
1916–1918
ISBN 1 84176 348 9
June 2002

The First World War
(4) The Mediterranean
Front 1914–1923
ISBN 1 84176 373 X
July 2002

The Second World
War (2) The Eastern
Front 1941–1945
ISBN 1 84176 391 8
July 2002

The Mexican War
1846–1848
ISBN 1 84176 472 8
July 2002

The Wars of
Alexander the Great
ISBN 1 84176 473 6
July 2002

Praise for Essential Histories

'clear and concise' *History Today*

'an excellent series' *Military Illustrated*

'Osprey must be congratulated on Essential Histories' *Soldier*

'very useful, factual and educational' *Reference Reviews*

'valuable as an introduction for students or younger readers … older readers will also find something 'essential'
to their understanding' *Star Banner*

'accessible and well illustrated…' *Daily Express*

'… clearly written …' *Oxford Times*

'they make the perfect starting point for readers of any age' *Daily Mail*

FIND OUT MORE ABOUT OSPREY

☐ Please send me a FREE trial issue of Osprey Military Journal

☐ Please send me the latest listing of Osprey's publications

☐ I would like to subscribe to Osprey's e-mail newsletter

Title/rank

Name

Address

Postcode/zip

State/country

E-mail

Which book did this card come from?

☐ I am interested in military history

My preferred period of military history is_____

☐ I am interested in military aviation

My preferred period of military aviation is _____

I am interested in (please tick all that apply)

☐ general history   ☐ militaria   ☐ model making

☐ wargaming   ☐ re-enactment

Please send to:

USA & Canada:
Osprey Direct USA, c/o Motorbooks International,
PO Box 1, 729 Prospect Avenue, Osceola, WI 54020, USA

UK, Europe and rest of world:
Osprey Direct UK, PO Box 140, Wellingborough,
Northants, NN8 2FA, United Kingdom

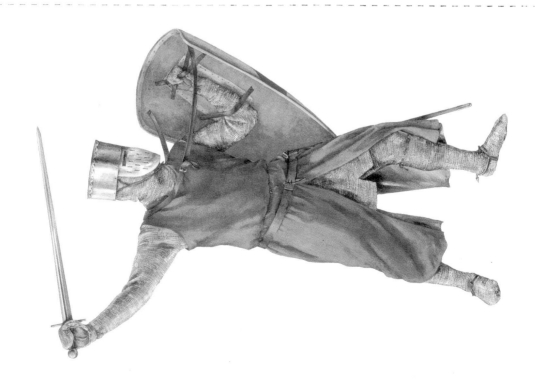

OSPREY
PUBLISHING

www.ospreypublishing.com

call our telephone hotline
for a free information pack

USA & Canada: 1-800-458-0454
UK, Europe and rest of world call:
+44 (0) 1933 443 863

Young Guardsman
Figure taken from *Warrior 22:*
Imperial Guardsman 1799–1815
Published by Osprey
Illustrated by Richard Hook

Knight, c.1190
Figure taken from *Warrior 1: Norman Knight 950 – 1204AD*
Published by Osprey
Illustrated by Christa Hook

POSTCARD